AN INDIAN HOUSEWIFE'S RECIPE BOOK

AN INDIAN HOUSEWIFE'S RECIPE BOOK

Laxmi Khurana

RIGHT WAY

Printed and bound in Great Britain by Cox & Wyman Ltd., Reading, Berkshire.

The *Right Way* series is published by Elliot Right Way Books, Brighton Road, Lower Kingswood, Tadworth, Surrey, KT20 6TD, U.K. For information about our company and the other books we publish, please visit our website at www.right-way.co.uk

PREFACE

The author is an Indian housewife, living in Britain. She enjoys cooking and has made it one of her particular hobbies and interests. When entertaining friends she has often heard remarks to the effect that Indian cooking is complicated, time-consuming and very difficult. This is not true. Indian cooking can be fun and simple. This book removes the myths, and explains Indian cooking by straightforward step by step methods. Many of the recipes in the book are for 'family' dishes which would not be served in restaurants. Hence the title 'An Indian House-wife's Recipe Book'.

ACKNOWLEDGEMENTS

Writing a book while in full time employment is not easy. My family and especially my children have shown a lot of patience and given me every encouragement. My children and many of my friends have been guinea pigs for testing the recipes. I would therefore like to thank all my friends for their efforts, and the question – Why don't you write a book? This is basically what started it.

So I would like to dedicate the book to my two children Micky and Reeta and my husband, without whose efforts this book would have never seen completion.

CONTENTS

INTRODUCTION

Indian food, and spicy food in general, has become common and increasingly popular outside India over the past few years. This is especially true in the U.K., where cosmopolitan influences have increased the number of non-English restaurants considerably. In spite of all this, there remains a myth that Indian cooking is cumbersome and time-consuming. This book explains how Indian cooking can be simple, based on a few, well-known spices which are easily available.

For simplicity I have divided Indian cooking into a number of sections; starters; savoury snacks; meat and fish curries; dhals; vegetable curries; chutneys, pickles and raitas; sundries, like chapattis, rice etc; and sweets. Starters and meat curry dishes are pretty standard, and easily understood by most people. However, the dhals and vegetable curries offer a lot of variety and are much used in Indian homes, but are not readily available in restaurants. Therefore, besides covering the more popular meat and sundry cookery, this book covers a range of dhal and vegetable dishes to give you the opportunity of trying them.

Utensils and Equipment

Here are some basic utensils and equipment needed for Indian cooking:-

a tava – heavy-based flat pan which can be bought at most Indian shops. If this is not available, then a large heavy-

based frying pan can be used.
a liquidiser or food processor
a sieve or skimmer (used for deep frying foods)
a wok, or a large, deep frying pan
a colander
a large serving spoon (the sort with spoon measurements marked on it).

In India, and in many restaurants in the U.K., a tandoor is often used. The tandoor is a clay oven, which is heated to a very high temperature in excess of 800°F (430°C). Most Indian homes in the U.K. do not have a tandoor, and therefore normally use an ordinary oven for tandoori dishes.

Ingredients

Some of the commonly used ingredients include:- tandoori masala, garam masala, madras curry powder, garlic, ginger (both fresh and powdered), chilli powder, turmeric powder, hing (asafoetida), coriander (fresh, seeds and powdered), black peppercorns, cinnamon, cardamom, cloves, nutmeg, cumin (both seeds and powdered), fennel seeds, fenugreek seeds, rai (both black mustard seeds and powder), soy sauce and ghee.

Tandoori masala, garam masala and madras curry powder are mixtures of other spices.

Tandoori masala is a combination of salt, coriander, cardamom powder, cinnamon powder, black peppercorns, cumin powder, ground cloves, chilli powder, ground bayleaves, mace, nutmeg, fenugreek powder, garlic powder and ginger powder. It is easily available in most large supermarkets.

Garam masala is a combination of coriander powder, cumin powder, black peppercorns, ginger powder, cinnamon powder, pimento, cardamom powder, ground bayleaves, ground cloves and nutmeg. This again is easily available in large supermarkets.

Madras curry powder, again very easily available from most supermarkets, is a mixture of cumin powder, chillies, turmeric powder, ground mustard seeds, ground poppy seeds, garlic powder, and ground fenugreek.

Ginger is available in both fresh and powder form, and is a reddish-brown coloured root. To use fresh ginger, remove the skin of the root and then chop finely. In powdered form, the root is first dried and then ground. Ginger can be purchased already powdered.

Garlic, again, is available in both fresh and powdered form. It is a very strong-smelling bulb, consisting of a number of small sections, known as cloves of garlic. To use fresh garlic, remove the skin from the clove, and chop finely. For the powdered form, the garlic is dried and then ground, or it can be purchased already powdered.

Chilli powder is often available in varying degrees of hotness. I recommend that milder forms of chilli powder are used initially. After some time, when you really want to try extra hot dishes, then either use slightly larger quantities of mild chilli powder, or buy a hotter variety.

Fresh green chillies are used in many recipes. If these are chopped by hand (rather than a liquidiser or food processor), you should make sure that you wash your hands with soap immediately after cutting them. This is essential because otherwise a burning sensation will be felt on your hands. This sensation transfers to any other part of your body that you touch. Fresh green chillies are available at most supermarkets.

Turmeric powder is the powdered form of the stem of a plant. It is bright yellow in colour and is widely available.

Hing (asafoetida) is a gum resin which is available either in gum or powder form. It has a very strong smell, and is mainly used for flavouring. It also aids digestion. It is available in most Indian shops but is not generally found in supermarkets. Some of the curries in this book use hing, but if it is not available, then the curry can be cooked without it. The fragrance of the curry will be less strong but only a small difference in taste is apparent.

Coriander is available in three forms: fresh, which is a green leaf used for garnishing and flavouring; powder, which is used for flavouring; and seeds, which are sometimes used for growing fresh coriander. Powdered coriander is easily available, but fresh coriander can be difficult to obtain. If it is not available then use fresh parsley for garnishing instead.

Black peppercorns are mainly used in savoury snacks and biryanis. It is the fruit of a plant and is easily obtainable in most supermarkets. Powdered form is often used in raitas and pickles.

Cinnamon is also available in two forms: cinnamon stick, which is the dried bark of the Asiatic shrub, broken into smaller pieces; and the powdered form, which can be used instead of the stick. The powdered form can be easily obtained.

Cardamom is a dried fruit with very aromatic seeds. Several of the seeds are enclosed together in a light green or creamish-white coloured pod. The pod can be used whole, or the seeds can be removed from the pods and then used.

Cloves are the dried flower buds of a special Asiatic tree. They are used whole, for flavouring, in many curries.

Nutmeg is the very hard, aromatic seed of a tree. The seeds are ground, and powdered nutmeg is easily available in most supermarkets.

Cumin is the dried fruit of an umbrella type of plant (umbelliferous), which is used for flavouring. Both the powdered form and the seeds are very widely used in curries and pickles. Both forms are easily available from supermarkets.

Fennel seeds, like cumin, are also a dried fruit. They are used in some recipes and for making tea. Fennel seeds, light green in colour, have a very mild bitter taste. They are also often eaten raw.

Fenugreek seeds are very dark orange in colour and are often used to grow fresh fenugreek. Ground fenugreek is used in making various mixed spices and in chutneys and pickles. Fresh fenugreek is a vegetable, sometimes cooked like spinach.

Rai (black mustard seeds) are the seeds from the pods of yellow flowers of a small plant. The seeds are used for flavouring curries, and the powdered form is used for pickles. Both varieties of rai are available from most Asian shops or large supermarkets. Sometimes health food shops also sell rai.

Soy sauce, an extract of soya beans, is not commonly used in India. Elsewhere, however, many Indian homes use it for cooking curries.

Ghee can be obtained from some Indian shops, but clarified butter could be used in its place. Clarified butter can be made by boiling unsalted butter itself for about 20 minutes, allowing it to cool, and then skimming off the scum on the surface to leave a clear liquid. If salted butter is used, then the clear liquid should be poured off, and the salt residue left in the pan. The clear liquid solidifies after cooling and is used for cooking. The residue is thrown away.

Most of these spices can be obtained in bulk, and stored in a cool place for up to nine months or a year. It is a lot cheaper to buy spices in this way than to buy an occasional two or four ounce packet. If you find it difficult to obtain garam masala, tandoori masala, madras curry powder or any of the other spices, there are a number of Indian shops which sell by post.

Marinating

In Indian cooking, the process of marinating is frequently used to flavour foods. Marinating is often done by soaking the food to be flavoured in a mixture of yoghurt and spices. The minimum amount of time for marinating is about four hours, but the longer you leave food marinating, the better it tastes. This is especially true of tandoori dishes, where the fresh meat needs to marinate for about eight to twelve hours. Marination also serves to tenderise meat.

Dhals

Dhals, often called pulses, are different types of seeds, used to make a variety of dishes. There are about fifteen different types of dhals; and again these can be bought in bulk and stored for up to a year. It is very difficult to describe all the different types of seeds in English; only a couple are well-known in English households, namely lentils and chickpeas. Most other varieties are available in Indian shops, and the Indian names may be used to buy them. Dhals are an acquired taste, and there is a tremendous variety in the way they can be cooked and, accordingly, in their flavour. They are usually served with rice, or another curry. Care must be taken in cooking dhals, to ensure that the seeds are well-boiled. They should not be eaten raw. This is because, unless cooked properly, they can be difficult to digest. In all the dhal recipes, cooking times should be carefully adhered to.

Different types of dhals are often ground to make flour. This flour is used to make poppadums, dhokra and a variety of other dishes. Also used in Indian cooking are two very commonly used flours, besan, or gram, flour, and chapatti flour. Besan flour is made from ground black grams, which are pulses. Chapatti flour is made from ground wheat. Neither of these flours has a direct English equivalent, but are easily obtainable from Indian shops, or health food stores.

Dhals often contain impurities like dust particles and

chaff. So before they are cooked, they need to be washed properly. This is done in one of the following two ways:-

The seeds can be individually sorted out, a few at a time and the impurities individually picked out. This method is the best, but is very laborious and time-consuming.

A faster method which is nearly as successful is to wash the dhal in such a way that the impurities sink to the bottom or float to the top. This is done by taking two large pans and placing the dhal in one of them. Add plenty of cold water so that it covers the dhal by about two inches. Now shake the pan so as to stir the dhal. The chaff floats to the top and can be thrown away. Transfer the rest of the contents gradually to the second pan until very little dhal is left in the first pan. The impurities should be at the bottom with this small amount of dhal. This residue can either be discarded with the impurities or carefully picked so that all the impurities are thrown away. Repeat this process of mixing fresh water, stirring and transferring the contents back and forth about six to seven times. This method has something in common with the principles of 'gold panning' in olden times.

Vegetables

There is a tremendous variety of vegetable dishes in Indian cooking. Most of the vegetables are sold in English shops, e.g. potatoes, peas, aubergines, okra and peppers. The book does, however, include recipes which contain four rather uncommon vegetables. These are tindora, vallour, kadu and guaer. These are available from most Indian shops, and obviously have to be bought fresh. The closest approximation to any one of these four special vegetables is marrow, which can be used instead of kadu. These uncommon dishes are well worth a try if you enjoy experimenting and are vegetarian. The Indian names can be used to buy these vegetables.

Raitas

Raitas are made from fresh natural yoghurt. Most Indian households make their own natural yoghurt, and raitas always taste better with freshly made yoghurt. Obviously they are not a main meal, but could be described as sundry dishes.

Pickles and Chutneys

Pickles and chutneys are always available at the table – in fact, an Indian meal would be incomplete without a variety of them. You can buy many ready-made pickles from most English supermarkets, or else prepare your own, as shown in some of the recipes.

Quantities of Ingredients

Indian cooking is an acquired art. You can never be very precise about the quantity of spices; it depends very much on your own taste. Sometimes it is worth experimenting with quantities until you arrive at the blend which suits your own taste buds. It is always best to start with a minimum of spices, as I do in this book. After a while, perhaps you might like to add other spices to the recipes in very small quantities, to experiment with flavours. You should not be afraid to do this, as all Indian cooking has been handed down through the generations, each generation varying the blends of spices in its own way. In most Indian households today, the same curry cooked on different days may well taste slightly different. The measurements of spices in this book should therefore be used more as basic guidelines, rather than as hard and fast rules.

Since this book is mainly aimed at the reader who is cooking for a family, I have constructed most of the recipes as enough to feed four people. If the dining table is to be shared by a larger, or by a smaller number, then the amount of each ingredient must be increased, or reduced, proportionately.

Some ingredients like bay leaves and cloves are used for cooking but not eaten. The curry is served with these ingredients left in, but the person eating discards them at the side of the plate.

Preparation and Cooking Times

For convenience I have included a preparation and cooking time for each recipe. This is the total period from the moment of beginning work on the recipe until the time the food is to be served. Some of these times are quite long – several hours in a few instances. Of course this does not mean that the housewife is busy for hours just to make the one meal! The preparation and cooking times include the periods during which the ingredients are soaking or marinating – an important procedure which imparts the characteristic flavour to many Indian recipes. But these times do indicate to the busy housewife whether a particular recipe can be ready for supper tonight!

Serving the meal

As a final note, you may be interested to know how a typical Indian meal would be served. Usually, it would start with drinks, and an assortment of savoury snacks, whilst sitting around before dinner. Once at the table, the meal typically begins with a starter, and this is followed by one or two meat dishes, accompanied by a rice dish with one vegetable curry and/or dhal. Chapattis or parothas or puris are also served at the same time, but usually only one of the options is served. Raitas, poppadums and a variety of pickles and chutneys should also be placed on the table, together with a fresh salad. Normally, as the dishes are laid out, the diners help themselves to a selection of each as they require. Drinks to accompany Indian meals are usually non-alcoholic, as the spicy food tends to detract from the flavour of wine, and vice versa. Therefore, either iced water with a slice of lemon and a small amount of sugar is served, or lassi (yoghurt and water combined). However, wine or beer can be served, according to individual taste. Once the main course is finished, the sweet is served, followed by coffee or tea. Indian tea is made by adding tea, a teaspoonful of fennel seeds and 2 or 3 cardamoms to water, bringing the water to the boil and boiling for about 3 to 4 minutes, adding milk and boiling again for about 2 to 3 minutes, thus making a strong brew of tea. This is usually served, accompanied by fennel seeds mixed with sugar crystals, on a plate. This should give you some guidelines, if you are planning on having a full Indian meal, on how to serve, and what dishes to combine.

1 STARTERS

ONION BHAJIS
(Onion Rings fried in gram flour batter)

This is one of the many Indian starter dishes. It can also be used as a snack served with a glass of wine etc. For this recipe you will need a liquidiser and a deep frying pan or wok.

Ingredients   *Serves 4*

½ oz (10g) fresh ginger (peeled)
½ oz (10g) fresh garlic (peeled)
4 green chillies
3 oz (85g) besan flour (gram flour)
½ tsp salt
½ tsp chilli powder
½ tsp garam masala
½ tsp tandoori masala

(continued overleaf)

(contd from p. 21)

3 fl oz (90ml) water
2 largish onions, cut into rings
20 fl oz (600ml) cooking oil for deep frying

Method   *Preparation and cooking time: 40 mins.*

1. Put the ginger, garlic and green chillies into a liquidiser and process until very finely chopped.

2. Sieve the gram flour into a mixing bowl. Add the contents of the liquidiser, salt, chilli powder, garam masala, tandoori masala and mix well. Add the water and mix well again into a thickish, smooth batter.

3. Add the onion rings to the batter and mix gently so that the onions are well covered with batter.

4. Heat the oil to a high temperature in a small wok, or deep frying pan. When the oil is hot, remove the onion rings one at a time from the batter and deep fry in the oil. This method of frying onions is similar to frying chips or fish in batter. Fry only 6 to 7 rings at a time.

5. Serve the onion bhajis while they are still hot.

POTATO PAKORAS
(Thinly sliced potatoes in gram flour batter)

This is another savoury snack which can be served at high teas. It is also a good starter to a main meal. Potato lovers will enjoy this dish. Most children are very fond of potato pakoras. For this recipe you need a deep frying pan or wok.

Ingredients   *Serves 4*

6 oz (170g) besan flour (gram flour)
4 fl oz (120ml) water

12 oz (340g) potatoes, peeled and sliced finely, similar to crisps, but slightly thicker
¾ tsp garlic powder
¾ tsp salt
¾ tsp chilli powder
¾ tsp garam masala
¾ tsp turmeric powder
20 fl oz (600ml) cooking oil for frying

Method　　　　*Preparation and cooking time: 30 mins.*

1. Sieve the gram flour into a mixing bowl.

2. Mix the flour, water, potatoes, garlic powder, salt, chilli powder, garam masala, and turmeric powder well.

3. Heat the cooking oil to a high temperature in a wok or deep frying pan. Pick each potato piece individually from the mixture and place it in the hot oil until you have about 10 pieces. The pakoras will float in the oil, and each side should be deep fried until it is golden orange. With a sieve, drain the pakoras.

4. Repeat with the remaining pakoras and serve while hot.

SPINACH PAKORAS
(Sliced spinach in gram flour batter)

This is another savoury snack which can be served at high teas. It is also a good starter to a main meal. Spinach lovers will really enjoy spinach pakoras. For this recipe you need a deep frying pan or wok.

Ingredients　　　　　　　　　　　　　*Serves 4*
4 oz (110g) besan flour (gram flour)
2 oz (55g) spinach, finely chopped
3 fl oz (90ml) water
¾ tsp salt

(continued overleaf)

(contd from p. 23)

¾ tsp chilli powder
3 green chillies, finely chopped
¾ tsp turmeric powder
20 fl oz (600ml) cooking oil for frying

Method   *Preparation and cooking time: 30 mins.*

1. Sieve the gram flour into a mixing bowl.

2. Mix the flour, spinach, water, salt, chilli powder, chillies and tumeric powder well.

3. Heat cooking oil to a high temperature in a wok or deep frying pan. Take a teaspoonful of the spinach mixture and place it gently in the hot oil. Repeat this until you have about 10 pieces. After a few seconds the pieces will float to the top of the oil. Then fry each side of the spinach pakora until it is golden orange. This frying process should take about 4 to 5 minutes, otherwise the oil is too hot and therefore the heat should be lowered. With a sieve, drain the pakoras and place them on kitchen roll paper.

4. Repeat with the remaining spinach mixture.

5. Transfer the pakoras to a serving dish and serve while hot.

MIXED PAKORAS

(Onions, potatoes and spinach in gram flour batter)

This is another savoury dish which can be used as a starter or a snack. It can also be served with high teas or at parties. For this recipe you will need a liquidiser or blender and a deep frying pan or wok.

Ingredients   *Serves 4*

½ oz (10g) fresh garlic (peeled)
½ oz (10g) fresh ginger (peeled)

5 green chillies
6 oz (170g) besan flour (gram flour)
2 potatoes, peeled and finely chopped
3 oz (85g) fresh spinach, finely chopped
1 large onion, finely chopped
1 tsp chilli powder
1 tsp tandoori masala
1 tsp garam masala
1 tsp salt
1 tsp turmeric powder
4 fl oz (120ml) water
20 fl oz (600ml) cooking oil for frying

Method   *Preparation and cooking time: 40 mins.*

1. Put the garlic, ginger and green chillies into a liquidiser and chop finely.

2. Sieve the gram flour into a mixing bowl and mix in the contents of the liquidiser, potatoes, spinach, onion, chilli powder, tandoori masala, garam masala, salt, turmeric powder and water. Mix everything well.

3. Heat the oil to a high temperature in a wok or deep frying pan. Add about 10 tablespoonfuls of the mixture, a tablespoonful at a time, to the heated oil. These will float and should be deep fried for about 3 to 4 minutes, until each of the fried pakoras is golden brown.

4. Remove the pakoras with a sieve and drain the excess oil off them by placing the pakoras on kitchen roll paper.

5. Repeat with the remaining pakoras and serve while hot.

CHICKEN PAKORAS
(Chicken pieces in gram flour batter)

This is another savoury snack which can be served at high teas, parties or even picnics. For this recipe you need a deep frying pan or wok.

Ingredients   *Serves 4*

1 lb (450g) frozen chicken pieces (thawed)
4 oz (110g) besan flour (gram flour)
4 fl oz (120ml) water
½ tsp salt
½ tsp chilli powder
½ tsp garam masala
½ tsp turmeric powder
2 tsp soy sauce
20 fl oz (600ml) cooking oil for frying

Method   *Preparation and cooking time: 1 hr.*

1. Remove the skin of the chicken pieces and cut the flesh from the bones. Cut the flesh into about 1 inch (2cm) cubes.

2. Bake these chicken cubes in a preheated oven at a temperature of mark 4 (350°F or 180°C) for about 20 minutes. Remove the pieces from the oven and allow them to cool.

3. Sieve the gram flour into a mixing bowl.

4. Mix the flour, water, salt, chilli powder, garam masala, turmeric powder, and soy sauce well to form a thickish paste.

5. Heat the cooking oil to a high temperature in a wok or deep frying pan. Dip each chicken piece individually in the paste and place it in the hot oil until you have about 5 pieces. After a few seconds the chicken pakoras will float to the top of the oil. Deep fry each side of the pakora until it is golden orange. This will usually take about 2 minutes for each side. With a sieve, drain the pakoras.

6. Repeat with the remaining chicken pieces and serve while hot.

FISH PAKORAS

(Fish pieces in gram flour batter)

This is another savoury snack which can be served at high teas, parties or even picnics. It could also be served with chips, instead of the traditional English fish and chips. For this recipe you need a deep frying pan or wok.

Ingredients   *Serves 4*

1 lb (450g) of cod fillets
4 oz (110g) besan flour (gram flour)
4 fl oz (120ml) water
½ tsp salt
½ tsp chilli powder
½ tsp garam masala
½ tsp turmeric powder
2 tsp soy sauce
20 fl oz (600ml) cooking oil for frying

Method   *Preparation and cooking time: 1 hr.*

1. Cut the fillets into about 2 inch (5cm) long and about ½ inch (1cm) wide pieces.

2. Sieve the gram flour into a mixing bowl.

3. Mix the flour, water, salt, chilli powder, garam masala, turmeric powder, and soy sauce well to form a thickish paste.

4. Heat the cooking oil to a high temperature in a wok or deep frying pan. Lower the heat and leave it for a further 3 to 4 minutes. Dip each fish piece individually in the paste and place it in the hot oil until you have about 5 pieces. After a few seconds the fish pakoras will float to the top of the oil. Deep fry each side of the pakora until it is golden orange. This will usually take about 4 minutes for each side. With a sieve, drain the fish pakoras.

5. Repeat with the remaining fish pieces and serve while hot.

VEGETABLE SAMOSAS
(Indian vegetable pasties)

This is a savoury snack served at parties or with high teas. It is useful for picnics too, because samosas are tasty even when cold. Raw filled samosas can be stored in a freezer and then fried when needed. For this recipe you need a flat frying pan or tava, and a deep frying pan or wok.

Ingredients   *Makes about 16 samosas*

For filling
1 lb (450g) potatoes
2 fl oz (60ml) cooking oil
½ tsp whole jeera (cumin seeds)
½ tsp whole rai (black mustard seeds)
1 large onion, finely chopped
4 oz (110g) frozen peas
1 tsp salt
½ tsp chilli powder
½ tsp tandoori masala
½ tsp turmeric powder
½ tsp garam masala
½ fl oz (15ml) lemon juice

For pastry
4 fl oz (120ml) water
8 oz (225g) plain flour
½ fl oz (15ml) lemon juice
A pinch of salt
2 oz (55g) plain flour (for rolling pastry)

For paste
1 oz (25g) plain flour

3 fl oz (90ml) water
20 fl oz (600ml) cooking oil for frying

Method   Preparation and cooking time: 1 hr. 20 mins.

1. Peel the potatoes and then boil them for about 10 minutes.

2. Cut the boiled potatoes into very small pieces.

3. Heat the 2 fluid ounces of oil in a frying pan, and add the jeera, rai, and chopped onion. Cook until the onion is golden brown. Add the potatoes, peas, salt, chilli powder, tandoori masala, turmeric powder, garam masala and lemon juice. Mix all the ingredients well, cook for about 2 minutes and remove the contents from the heat.

4. Mix the 4 fluid ounces of water, the 8 ounces of plain flour, the ½ fluid ounce of lemon juice and the pinch of salt into a medium soft dough.

5. Heat a 'tava', or a large flat frying pan, to a high temperature.

6. Divide the dough into 8 roughly equal parts and shape them into round balls. Sprinkle a little bit of the plain flour on to each ball. Roll each ball out flat (like a chapatti), about 7 to 8 inches (20cm) in diameter. Cook each side on the 'tava' for about 4 seconds.

7. Cut all the cooked chapattis into halves.

8. Now mix the 1 ounce of plain flour and the 2 fluid ounces of water thoroughly, until the mixture is like glue.

9. Take each half of the rolled chapatti, and form a cone by bringing its two corners together and joining the straight sides together with the paste. Now fill each of the cones with about 2 to 3 tablespoonfuls of the potato mixture and paste together the round ends of the cone. These filled cones are called samosas. Repeat with all the remaining chapattis.

10. These samosas can now be stored in a freezer for a period of up to 6 weeks. If stored in a freezer, they must be thawed for about 1 hour before deep frying.

11. Heat the 20 fluid ounces of oil in a wok or a large pan, and deep fry all the samosas, 4 to 5 at a time, until they are golden brown.

12. Serve the samosas hot, with tomato ketchup.

BEEF SAMOSAS
(Indian beef pasties)

This is a savoury snack served at parties or with high teas. Like vegetable samosas it is useful for picnics. Raw filled samosas can be stored in a freezer and then fried when needed. For this recipe you need a flat frying pan or tava and a deep frying pan or wok.

Ingredients   *Makes about 16 samosas*

For filling
1 fl oz (30ml) cooking oil
½ tsp whole rai (black mustard seeds)
½ tsp whole jeera (cumin seeds)
1 small onion, finely chopped
8 oz (225g) minced beef
2 oz (55g) finely chopped potatoes
2 oz (55g) finely chopped fresh carrots
½ tsp salt
1 tsp turmeric powder
1 tsp chilli powder
1 fl oz (30ml) lemon juice

For pastry
4 fl oz (120ml) water
8 oz (225g) plain flour
½ fl oz (15ml) lemon juice

A pinch of salt

2 oz (55g) plain flour (for rolling)

For paste
1 oz (25g) plain flour
2 fl oz (60ml) water

20 fl oz (600ml) cooking oil for frying

Method   *Preparation and cooking time: 1 hr. 30 mins.*

1. Heat the 1 fluid ounce of oil in a frying pan to a high temperature, and add the rai, jeera, and the chopped onion. Cook until the onion is golden brown. Add the mince, potatoes, carrots, salt, turmeric powder and chilli powder. Mix all the ingredients well, lower the heat and cover the pan. Simmer the mixture for about 20 minutes stirring every 10 minutes. Now add the 1 fluid ounce of lemon juice, switch off the heat and leave the contents to cool.

2. Mix the 4 fluid ounces of water, the 8 ounces of plain flour, the ½ fluid ounce of lemon juice and the pinch of salt into a medium soft dough.

3. Heat a 'tava' or a large flat frying pan to a high temperature.

4. Divide the dough into 8 roughly equal parts and shape them into round balls. Sprinkle a little bit of the plain flour on to each of the balls. Roll out each ball flat (like a chapatti), about 7 to 8 inches (20cm) in diameter. Cook each side on the 'tava' for about 4 seconds.

5. Cut all the cooked chapattis into halves.

6. Now mix the 1 ounce of plain flour and the 2 fluid ounces of water thoroughly, until the mixture is like glue.

7. Take each half of the rolled chapatti, and form a cone by bringing its two corners together and joining the

straight sides together with the paste. Now fill each of the cones with about 2 to 3 tablespoonfuls of the beef mixture and paste together the round ends of the cone. These filled cones are called samosas. Repeat with all the remaining chapattis.

8. These samosas can now be stored in a freezer for a period of up to 6 weeks. If stored in a freezer, they must be thawed for about 1 hour before deep frying.

9. Heat the 20 fluid ounces of oil in a wok or a large pan, and deep fry all the samosas, 4 to 5 at a time, until they are golden brown.

10. Serve the samosas hot, with tomato ketchup.

TANDOORI SPARE RIB PORK CHOPS WITH SALAD

This is usually served as a mild starter. It can be used as a main dish, served with pilaw rice. During summer days, it makes an excellent addition to salad, instead of ham or cold chicken. For this recipe you can either buy small (about 3 inch long) pork chops or get your butcher to cut large chops into halves. You will require a liquidiser for this recipe.

Ingredients   *Serves 4*

3 fl oz (90ml) plain yoghurt
1 tsp salt
1 tsp turmeric powder
2 tsp tomato purée
2 tsp tandoori masala
2 oz (55g) fresh garlic (peeled)
½ tsp chilli powder
2 oz (55g) fresh ginger (peeled)
4 green chillies

5–6 drops red food colouring
2 lb (900g) small spare rib pork chops
2 fl oz (60ml) cooking oil

For salad
3 oz (85g) cucumber slices
1 small onion, sliced
1 large fresh tomato, sliced
4 oz (110g) sliced radish (cut for salad)
1 lettuce, washed
1 lemon, sliced

Method   *Preparation and cooking time: 5 hrs. 30 mins.*

1. Place the yoghurt, salt, turmeric powder, tomato purée, tandoori masala, garlic, chilli powder, ginger, green chillies and red colouring into a liquidiser and blend into a liquid.

2. Place the pork pieces in a large bowl, and pour the contents of the liquidiser over the pieces. Allow the meat to marinate in the mixture for the next 4 hours.

3. Place a wire rack in a baking tray. (The wire stand in the grill tray is very useful for this.)

4. Remove all the pork pieces from the mixture and place them on the wire rack.

5. Spread the 2 fluid ounces of oil evenly over all the pork pieces.

6. Cook at mark 5 (375°F or 190°C), on the middle shelf of a preheated oven, for about 45 minutes. Turn the pork pieces, remove all the excess liquid from the tray, and cook for a further 45 minutes. The excess liquid should be thrown away.

7. Take a large serving dish. Arrange the salad and lemon

around the edge, and place the pork pieces in the middle of the salad.

8. Serve while the chops are still hot.

TANDOORI CHICKEN

This is a mild chicken starter. It can be served cold or hot and is very useful for picnics. You will require a liquidiser or blender for this recipe.

Ingredients   *Serves 4*

2 lb (900g) chicken pieces
3 fl oz (90ml) plain yoghurt
5–6 drops of red food colouring
1 tsp salt
1 tsp turmeric powder
3 tsp tomato purée
2 tsp tandoori masala
2 oz (55g) fresh garlic (peeled)
2 oz (55g) fresh ginger (peeled)
5 green chillies
2 fl oz (60ml) cooking oil

Method   *Preparation and cooking time: 6 hrs.*

1. Remove the skin from the chicken pieces. Place these pieces in a large pan.

2. Mix the yoghurt, food colouring, salt, turmeric powder, tomato purée, tandoori masala, garlic, ginger, and green chillies into a liquidiser and blend into a liquid. Pour this liquid over the chicken pieces.

3. Leave the mixture to marinate for 4 to 6 hours.

4. Place a wire rack in a baking tray. (The wire stand in the grill tray is very useful for this). Remove the chicken pieces from the mixture and arrange them on the wire

rack. Spread the cooking oil evenly on the chicken.

5. Cook at mark 5 (375°F or 190°C) in the middle shelf of a preheated oven, for about 30 minutes. Remove all the excess liquid and carry on cooking for another 20 minutes. Remove any further excess liquid, turn the chicken pieces and cook for a further 30 minutes. All the excess liquid should be thrown away.

6. Place chicken in serving dish.

TANDOORI FISH WITH SALAD

This is an excellent mild starter for a special occasion. You will require a liquidiser or blender for this recipe.

Ingredients   *Serves 4*

4 fl oz (120ml) plain yoghurt
1 tsp salt
1 tsp turmeric powder
2 tsp tomato purée
2 tsp tandoori masala
1 oz (25g) fresh garlic (peeled)
1 oz (25g) fresh ginger (peeled)
5–6 drops red food colouring
4 green chillies
1½ lb (675g) cod fish, cut into 4 inch (10cm) long pieces
2 fl oz (60ml) cooking oil

For salad
4 oz (110g) cucumber slices
1 onion, sliced
2 fresh tomatoes (cut for salad)
4 oz (110g) sliced radish (cut for salad)
Some fresh lettuce, washed
1 lemon, sliced

Method   *Preparation and cooking time: 2 hrs. 45 mins.*

1. Place the yoghurt, salt, turmeric powder, tomato purée, tandoori masala, garlic, ginger, food colouring and green chillies into a liquidiser and blend into a liquid.

2. Place the fish pieces in a large pan. Pour the blended liquid over the fish and let the mixture marinate for about 2 hours.

3. Place a wire rack in a baking tray. (The wire stand in the grill tray is very useful for this.)

4. Remove all the fish pieces from the pan and place them on the wire rack.

5. Spread the oil evenly on the fish pieces.

6. Cook at mark 5 (375°F or 190°C) on the middle shelf of a preheated oven for about 35 minutes.

7. Arrange the salad and lemon around the sides of a large serving dish and place the fish in the centre.

8. Serve while the fish is hot.

BEEF KEBABS

The word *kebab* has a different meaning in Indian cookery. Indian kebabs are like burgers and are made of mince mixed with spices. Beef kebabs are usually served as starters. They also make excellent snacks for high teas, parties and barbecues.

Ingredients   *Serves 4*

1 lb (450g) minced beef
1 large onion, finely chopped
1 tsp garam masala
1 tsp tomato purée
1 tsp salt
1 tsp tandoori masala

½ tsp chilli powder
1 tsp whóle jeera (cumin seeds)
5–6 drops red food colouring

Method   *Preparation and cooking time: 1 hr.*

1. Mix all the above ingredients thoroughly in a large mixing bowl.

2. Divide the mixture into about 8 equal parts.

3. Roll each part into a ball and then roll it flat, about ¼ inch (½cm) thick, 2 to 3 inches (7cm) in diameter, like a burger.

4. Grill each side for about 10 minutes under a hot grill.

5. Serve while hot.

LAMB KEBABS WITH SALAD

Lamb kebabs are made of minced lamb mixed with spices, and are usually served as a starter. They can also be served at parties or with a glass of wine, as a snack to accompany the drink. For this recipe you need a liquidiser.

Ingredients   *Serves 4*

1 oz (25g) fresh garlic (peeled)
1 oz (25g) fresh ginger (peeled)
4 green chillies
1 lb (450g) minced lamb
1 large onion, finely chopped
1 tsp salt
2 tsp tandoori masala
½ tsp chilli powder
1 tsp whole jeera (cumin seeds)
3 tsp tomato purée

(continued overleaf)

(contd from p. 37)

For salad
Fresh crispy lettuce
3 oz (85g) cucumber, sliced
1 small onion, sliced
2 fresh tomatoes, sliced for salad
1 lemon, sliced

Method   *Preparation and cooking time: 1 hr. 35 mins.*

1. Process the garlic, fresh ginger and green chillies in a liquidiser until finely chopped.

2. Mix the contents of the liquidiser, mince, onion, salt, tandoori masala, chilli powder, jeera and tomato purée in a large mixing bowl. Mix everything together well.

3. Divide the mixture into roughly 8 equal portions. Shape each of these portions into sausage type shapes. These shapes are called kebabs.

4. Place these kebabs on the wire stand of a grill pan and cook under a hot grill for about 25 minutes turning sides of the kebabs every 5 to 7 minutes. Take extreme care when changing sides so as not to break the kebabs.

5. Arrange the salad on one side of a serving dish, and arrange the cooked kebabs on the other side of the dish.

6. Serve while hot.

SPARE RIBS COOKED IN MICROWAVE OVEN

If you are fond of pork and want to try something new on the family or friends, then this dish is extremely useful. These spare ribs can be served with salad or rice. For this recipe you can either buy small spare ribs or get your butcher to cut large ribs into halves. This recipe needs a microwave oven and a deep frying pan or wok.

Ingredients   *Serves 4*

20 fl oz (600ml) cooking oil for frying
2 lb (900g) small spare ribs
2 tsp tomato purée
2 tsp tomato ketchup
1 tsp garlic powder
4 tsp soy sauce
3 fl oz (90ml) water

Method   *Preparation and cooking time: 40 mins.*

1. Heat the oil to a high temperature in a wok or deep frying pan and then deep fry the ribs until they are golden brown. This will usually take about 15 to 20 minutes.

2. Transfer the fried meat into a 10 inch (25cm) pyrex or microwave dish.

3. Mix the tomato purée, tomato ketchup, garlic powder, soy sauce and water together and pour the mixture on top of the ribs. Place the dish in a microwave oven and cook for 10 minutes at full power.

4. Serve while hot.

TOMATO SOUP

Indian tomato soup is a heavily spiced version of English tomato soup. It is one of the few vegetarian starters in Indian cookery and is a very light and thin soup. Like all soups, it can be served with bread or a roll.

Ingredients   *Serves 4*

1 lb (450g) ripe tomatoes
1 fl oz (30ml) cooking oil

(continued overleaf)

(contd from p. 39)

6 whole cloves
½ tsp whole rai (black mustard seeds)
½ tsp hing (asafoetida)
1 tsp salt
1 tsp turmeric powder
1 tsp chilli powder
2 tsp sugar
15 fl oz (450ml) water

Method   *Preparation and cooking time: 20 mins.*

1. Wash all the tomatoes and cut them into very small pieces.

2. Heat the oil in a pan and add cloves, whole rai and asafoetida. Fry for a few seconds.

3. Add the tomatoes, salt, turmeric powder, chilli powder and the sugar. Reduce the heat, cover the pan and simmer gently for about 7 minutes.

4. Now add the water, mix well and bring to the boil. Allow it to simmer for a further 10 minutes.

5. Transfer the soup to a soup bowl; remove the cloves with a spoon and serve while hot.

POTATO KACHORIS

(Potato balls in chapatti flour)

This dish is very similar to samosas, but the pastry is made of chapatti flour, rather than plain flour. It can be served as a starter or at high teas and parties. Any left-over filling can be used for toasted sandwiches. For this recipe you need a deep frying pan or wok.

Ingredients   *Makes about 8 kachoris*

For filling
1 fl oz (30ml) cooking oil
½ tsp whole rai (black mustard seeds)
1 large onion, finely chopped
1 lb (450g) peeled potatoes, finely diced
1 tsp salt
1 tsp turmeric powder
1 tsp chilli powder
2 fl oz (60ml) water
½ fl oz (15ml) lemon juice

For pastry

8 oz (225g) white chapatti flour, sieved
4 fl oz (120ml) water
2 oz (55g) chapatti flour for rolling out

20 fl oz (600ml) cooking oil for frying

Method   *Preparation and cooking time: 1 hr.*

1. In a pan, heat the oil to a high temperature. Add rai and let it cook for a few seconds. Add the onion and cook until the onion is golden brown. Add the potatoes, salt, turmeric powder and chilli powder. Stir and cook for about 2 minutes.

2. Add the 2 fluid ounces of water, lower the heat, cover the pan and allow it to simmer for about 10 minutes. Then add the lemon juice, mix well, and switch off the heat. Let it cool.

3. Place the chapatti flour in a big bowl; add half of the 4 fluid ounces of water and mix well. Continue adding small amounts of water at a time and mixing well until a soft, medium dough is formed. Divide this dough into roughly 8 equal pieces. Shape these pieces into round balls.

4. Sprinkle some dry flour onto each ball, and roll it into a circle about five inches (13cm) in diameter. Place 4 teaspoonsfuls of the potato filling in the middle of one half of the rolled chapatti. Lift the other half to cover the filling completely and squeeze the edges together thus making a semi-circle shape with the filling in the middle. Lift it carefully and place it on one side. Repeat this with all the 8 balls. These filled balls are called kachoris.

5. Heat the 20 fluid ounces of oil to a high temperature, in a deep frying pan or wok. Now add 2 kachoris at a time and fry each side of the kachori until it is golden brown. This will usually take about 3 to 4 minutes for each side. Fry all the kachoris in this way.

6. Serve the kachoris while they are hot.

MOONG KACHORIS
(Moong dhal balls in chapatti flour)

This dish is very similar to samosas, but the pastry is made of chapatti flour, rather than plain flour. Moong dhal kachoris are more popular with vegetarians. It can be served as a starter or at high teas and parties. Any left-over filling can be used for toasted sandwiches. For this recipe you need a deep frying pan or wok.

Ingredients   *Makes about 8 kachoris*
For filling
8 oz (225g) skinless, split moong dhal
40 fl oz (1200ml) of water for soaking
1 fl oz (30ml) cooking oil
½ tsp whole rai (black mustard seeds)
½ tsp whole jeera (cumin seeds)
1½ tsp salt
1 tsp turmeric powder
1 tsp chilli powder

1 tsp garam masala
10 fl oz (300ml) water
1 fl oz (30ml) lemon juice

For pastry
8 oz (225g) white chapatti flour, sieved
4 fl oz (120ml) water
2 oz (55g) chapatti flour for rolling out

20 fl oz (600ml) cooking oil for frying

Method   *Preparation and cooking time: 10 hrs.*

1. Wash the moong dhal making sure that little stones are not left in the dhal. (See page 16.)

2. Soak the dhal overnight in the 40 fluid ounces of water.

3. Drain the water from the dhal in the morning.

4. In a pan, heat the oil to a high temperature. Add rai and jeera and cook for a few seconds. Add the dhal, salt, turmeric powder, chilli powder and garam masala. Stir and cook for about 2 minutes.

5. Add the 10 fluid ounces of water, lower the heat, cover the pan and allow it to simmer for about 20 minutes. Now add the lemon juice, mix well and switch off the heat. Let this filling cool down.

6. Place the chapatti flour in a big bowl; add half of the 4 fluid ounces of water and mix well. Continue adding small amounts of water at a time and mixing well until a soft, medium dough is formed. Divide this dough into roughly 8 equal parts. Shape these parts into round balls.

7. Sprinkle some dry flour into the balls, and roll each ball into a 5 inch (13cm) diameter round shape. Place 4 teaspoonfuls of the moong dhal filling in the middle of one half of the rolled chapatti. Lift the other half to cover the filling completely and squeeze the edges together thus

making a semi-circle shape with the filling in the middle. Lift it carefully and place it on one side. Repeat this with all the 8 balls. These filled balls are called kachoris.

8. Heat the 20 fluid ounces of oil to a high temperature, in a deep frying pan or wok. Now add 2 kachoris at a time and fry each side of the kachori until it is golden brown. This will usually take about 3 to 4 minutes for each side. Fry all the kachoris in this way.

9. Serve the kachoris while they are hot.

PORK TIKKA

(Pork pieces, marinated and cooked in yoghurt)

All tikka dishes make very good starters and snacks. As starters they are usually served with a salad. For this recipe you need a liquidiser.

Ingredients   *Serves 4*

1 oz (25g) fresh garlic (peeled)
1 oz (25g) fresh ginger (peeled)
4 green chillies
6 fl oz (180ml) natural, fresh yoghurt
2 tsp soy sauce
1 tsp salt
2 tsp tomato purée
1 tsp turmeric powder
1 tsp chilli powder
1 tsp red food colouring
½ fl oz (15ml) lemon juice
12 oz (340g) pork steak
2 fl oz (60ml) cooking oil
4 fl oz (120ml) water

Method *Preparation and cooking time: 8 hrs. 50 mins.*

1. Mix the garlic, ginger, chillies, yoghurt, soy sauce, salt, tomato purée, turmeric powder, chilli powder, red food colouring and lemon juice in a liquidiser and blend it into a liquid.

2. Cut the pork steak into small ½ inch (1cm) cubes.

3. Place the pork pieces in a large pan and then pour the blended mixture on the pork pieces.

4. Leave the mixture to marinate for about 8 hours.

5. Heat the oil in a large pan to a high temperature and then add the pork with all its spiced liquid. Stir continuously and cook for about 10 minutes.

6. Add the 4 fluid ounces of water, cover the pan, lower the heat and let it simmer for about 35 minutes, stirring every 5 to 7 minutes.

7. Remove the cover of the pan, raise the heat and let the water evaporate, leaving a rather dry pork tikka. This will usually take about 3 to 4 minutes.

8. Serve hot, with salad or on its own.

CHICKEN TIKKA
(Chicken pieces, marinated and cooked in yoghurt)

All tikka dishes make very good starters and snacks. As starters they are usually served with a salad. For this recipe you need a liquidiser and a sharp knife.

Ingredients *Serves 4*

1 oz (25g) fresh garlic (peeled)
1 oz (25g) fresh ginger (peeled)
4 green chillies
6 fl oz (180ml) natural, fresh yoghurt

(continued overleaf)

(contd from p. 45)

2 tsp soy sauce
1 tsp salt
2 tsp tomato purée
1 tsp turmeric powder
1 tsp chilli powder
1 tsp red food colouring
½ fl oz (15 ml) lemon juice
1½ lb (670g) chicken pieces
2 fl oz (60ml) cooking oil
2 fl oz (60ml) water

Method   *Preparation and cooking time: 8 hrs. 40 mins.*

1. Place the garlic, ginger, chillies, yoghurt, soy sauce, salt, tomato purée, turmeric powder, chilli powder, red colouring and lemon juice in a liquidiser and blend into a liquid.

2. Remove the skin from the chicken pieces and chop into about 1 inch (2½cm) long pieces.

3. Place the chicken pieces in a large pan and pour over the blended mixture.

4. Leave this mixture to marinate for about 8 hours.

5. Heat the oil in a large pan to a high temperature and then add the chicken with all its spiced liquid. Stir continuously and cook for about 10 minutes.

6. Now add the 2 fluid ounces of water, cover the pan, lower the heat and let it simmer for about 25 minutes, stirring every 5 to 7 minutes.

7. Now remove the cover of the pan, raise the heat and let the water evaporate, leaving a rather dry chicken dish. This will usually take about 3 to 4 minutes.

8. Serve hot, with salad or on its own.

BEEF TIKKA

(Beef pieces, marinated and cooked in yoghurt)

All tikka dishes make very good starters and snacks. As starters they are usually served with a salad. For this recipe you need a liquidiser.

Ingredients   *Serves 4*

1 oz (25g) fresh garlic (peeled)
1 oz (25g) fresh ginger (peeled)
4 green chillies
6 fl oz (180ml) natural, fresh yoghurt
2 tsp soy sauce
1 tsp salt
2 tsp tomato purée
1 tsp turmeric powder
1 tsp chilli powder
1 tsp red food colouring
½ fl oz (15ml) lemon juice
12 oz (340g) beef steak
2 fl oz (60ml) cooking oil
6 fl oz (180ml) water

Method   *Preparation and cooking time: 9 hrs.*

1. Place the garlic, ginger, chillies, yoghurt, soy sauce, salt, tomato purée, turmeric powder, chilli powder, red colouring and lemon juice in a liquidiser and blend into a liquid.

2. Cut the beef steak into small, ½ inch (1cm) cubes.

3. Place the beef pieces in a large pan, and then pour the blended mixture onto the beef pieces.

4. Leave this mixture to marinate for about 8 hours.

5. Heat the oil in a large pan to a high temperature, and then add the beef with all its spiced liquid. Stir continuously, and cook for about 10 minutes.

6. Add the 6 fluid ounces of water, cover the pan, lower the heat and let it simmer for about 45 minutes, stirring every 5 to 7 minutes.

7. Remove the cover of the pan, raise the heat and let the water evaporate, leaving a rather dry beef dish. This will usually take about 3 to 4 minutes.

8. Serve hot, with salad or on its own.

LAMB TIKKA

(Lamb pieces, marinated and cooked in yoghurt)

All tikka dishes make very good starters and snacks. As starters they are usually served with a salad. For this recipe you need a liquidiser.

Ingredients   *Serves 4*

1 oz (25g) fresh garlic (peeled)
1 oz (25g) fresh ginger (peeled)
4 green chillies
6 fl oz (180ml) natural, fresh yoghurt
2 tsp soy sauce
1 tsp salt
2 tsp tomato purée
1 tsp turmeric powder
1 tsp chilli powder
1 tsp red food colouring
½ fl oz (15ml) lemon juice
12 oz (340g) diced lamb
2 fl oz (60ml) cooking oil
5 fl oz (150ml) water

Method   *Preparation and cooking time: 9 hrs.*

1. Place the garlic, ginger, chillies, yoghurt, soy sauce, salt, tomato purée, turmeric powder, chilli powder, red

colouring and lemon juice in a liquidiser and blend into a liquid.

2. Place the lamb pieces in a large pan, and pour the blended mixture onto the lamb pieces.

3. Leave this mixture to marinate for about 8 hours.

4. Heat the oil in a large pan to a high temperature and then add the lamb with all its spiced liquid. Stir continuously, and cook for about 10 minutes.

5. Add the 5 fluid ounces of water, cover the pan, lower the heat and let it simmer for about 40 minutes, stirring every 5 to 7 minutes.

6. Remove the cover of the pan, raise the heat and let the water evaporate, leaving a rather dry lamb dish. This will usually take about 3 to 4 minutes.

7. Serve hot, with salad or on its own.

2 SAVOURY SNACKS

MATHI

(A savoury biscuit made with plain flour)

This is a savoury biscuit, which is usually served with a cup of tea or coffee. It can also be used in packed lunches, picnics, or at parties. In fact it makes a good substitute for biscuits, especially if you like savoury snacks. Cooked mathis, like biscuits, can be stored in an airtight tin for up to 6 or 7 weeks. For this recipe you need a wok or deep frying pan.

Ingredients   *Makes about 60 mathis.*

1 lb (450g) plain flour
3 oz (85g) butter or soft margarine
½ tsp salt
1 tsp ground black pepper
3 fl oz (90ml) water
40 fl oz (1200ml) cooking oil for frying

Method   *Preparation and cooking time: 2 hrs.*

1. Sieve the plain flour into a large mixing bowl, and add the butter (or margarine), salt and ground pepper and mix well.

2. Mix in the water gradually until a medium soft dough is formed. (Make sure that you do not add too much water at a time).

3. Divide the mixture into little balls, about 1½ inches (4cm) in diameter.

4. Roll each ball into a circle about 3 inches (7cm) in diameter and about an eighth of an inch (2mm) thick.

5. Make a couple of 1 inch (2.5cm) marks on the rolled mathi, with a sharp knife. The knife should only penetrate the top and not cut through the whole thickness of the mathi.

6. Lay the rolled balls out separately.

7. Heat the oil in a wok or a deep frying pan to a high temperature. When it is hot, add about 3 mathis at a time and let them deep fry for a few seconds. Soon they will float to the top; now turn them and fry the mathis until they are golden brown all over. (The browning process on each mathi should take about 2 minutes; if it takes less time the oil is too hot and therefore the heat should be lowered.)

8. Let the mathis cool and then store them in an airtight tin.

VIDA

(A savoury snack made with corn flour)

This is an unusual snack, although common in the Gujarat state of India. For this recipe you need a deep frying pan, or wok, and a liquidiser.

Ingredients   *Serves 4*

8 oz (225g) cornflour
3 fl oz (90ml) yoghurt
4 fl oz (120ml) water
2 oz (55g) fresh garlic (peeled)
2 oz (55g) fresh ginger (peeled)
4 green chillies
½ tsp salt
½ tsp turmeric powder
½ tsp chilli powder
20 fl oz (600ml) cooking oil for frying

Method   Preparation and cooking time: 12 hrs. 40 mins.

1. Sieve the cornflour into a bowl. Add the yoghurt and mix well. Add water gradually and continue to mix until a stiff dough is formed. Cover the bowl and leave for about 12 hours.

2. Process the garlic, ginger and chillies in a liquidiser until finely chopped.

3. Add the salt, turmeric powder, chilli powder and liquidiser contents into the stiff dough. Mix everything together. Take a small amount of dough at a time; shape it first into a ball and then pat the ball into a circle about an inch and a half (4cm) in diameter and a quarter of an inch thick (½cm) thick. Wet the palms of your hands with water occasionally while doing this. These shapes are called vidas.

4. Heat the oil in a wok or deep frying pan to a high temperature, and fry the vidas (5 to 7 at a time) in the oil. Deep fry the vidas on a low heat. The frying process should take about 3–4 minutes; if it takes less then the oil is too hot. When the vidas are golden brown place them in a serving dish and serve while hot.

CHAVADA

(Mixture of many spiced nuts and seeds)

Chavada is a mixture of deep fried nuts and dhal, and is used as a savoury snack, usually served with a cup of tea or coffee. It can also be used in packed lunches, picnics or parties. Chavada can be stored in an airtight tin for about 4 to 5 weeks and used as and when needed. For this recipe you need a deep frying pan or wok.

Ingredients   *Makes about 3 lb of chavada*

1 lb (450g) chana dhal
40 fl oz (1200ml) cooking oil for frying
½ lb (225g) puffed rice
½ lb (225g) ready salted crisps
½ lb (225g) ready salted peanuts
1 tsp salt
1 tsp turmeric powder
1 tsp chilli powder

Method   *Preparation and cooking time: 12 hrs.*

1. Soak the chana dhal in about 70 fluid ounces (2 litres) of water overnight.

2. Drain off all the water from the dhal and spread on kitchen roll paper.

3. Heat the oil in a large wok, or frying pan to a high temperature. Place small amounts of dhal in the oil, and deep fry until the dhal seeds are golden brown, or eat one of the dhal seeds: it should taste hard and crunchy. Remove the dhal with a sieve and spread the fried dhal on some fresh kitchen roll paper. Fry all the dhal in this way.

4. Now fry the rice in the hot oil, again only a small quantity at a time. Puffed rice grains fry very quickly, so keep the pot and sieve ready.

5. Mix the fried rice, dhal, crisps, peanuts, salt, turmeric powder and chilli powder in a large pot. Mix well, and transfer the contents to an airtight tin. This will keep the chavada fresh for about a month.

6. Serve as and when needed, making sure that the lid of the tin is kept well closed, after use.

CHANA DHAL FRIED
(Deep fried gram seeds)

This is a deep fried gram dhal, usually served with a cup of tea or coffee. It can also be munched while watching television or just relaxing. Like chavada, fried chana dhal can be stored in an airtight tin for 4 to 5 weeks and used as and when needed. For this recipe you need a deep wok or frying pan.

Ingredients   *Makes about 2 lb of dhal*

2 lb (900g) chana dhal
40 fl oz (1200ml) cooking oil for frying
1 tsp salt
1 tsp turmeric powder
1 tsp chilli powder

Method   *Preparation and cooking time: 12 hrs.*

1. Soak the chana dhal in about 70 fluid ounces (2 litres) of water overnight.

2. Drain all the water from the dhal, and spread the dhal on some clean kitchen roll paper.

3. Heat the oil in a wok or deep frying pan to a high temperature. Add small amounts of the dhal to the oil and deep fry until the dhal seeds are golden brown. Another method of checking if they are ready is to eat one of the

dhal seeds. It should feel hard and crunchy. Remove the fried dhal with a sieve and spread it on some fresh clean kitchen roll paper. Repeat with the remaining dhal.

4. Add the salt, turmeric powder, and chilli powder to the dhal and mix well. Transfer the contents to an airtight tin. This will keep the dhal fresh for about a month.

HANDVA

(Spicy 'cake' type snack made from rice flour)

This is a savoury snack usually served at high teas, parties or picnics. It can be stored in the fridge for a couple of days and heated as and when required. For this recipe you need a liquidiser, a whisk and an 8 inch (20cm) cake tin.

Ingredients   *Serves 4*

3 fl oz (90ml) natural yoghurt
3 fl oz (90ml) water
12 oz (340g) of dhokra flour (mixture of ground rice and ground chana dhal, available from most Indian grocery shops)
1 oz (25g) fresh garlic (peeled)
3 green chillies
1 tsp salt
1 tsp turmeric powder
½ tsp chilli powder
¼ tsp baking powder
2 fl oz (60ml) cooking oil
¼ tsp whole jeera (cumin seeds)
¼ tsp whole rai (black mustard seeds)
¼ tsp hing (asafoetida)

Method   *Preparation and cooking time: 50 hrs.*

1. Mix the yoghurt and water together with a whisk. This mixture is called lassi.

2. Mix the dhokra flour and lassi together well, and leave to ferment in a warm spot, for 48 hours. The airing cupboard is ideal for this purpose.

3. Place the garlic and chillies into a liquidiser, and chop very finely.

4. After fermentation, add the salt, turmeric powder, chilli powder, baking powder and liquidiser contents to the dhokra mixture. Mix well.

5. Heat the oil in a frying pan to a high temperature, and add the jeera, rai and hing (asafoetida). Cook for a few seconds.

6. Transfer half of the heated oil mixture to an 8 inch (20cm) cake tin. Add the dhokra flour mixture and then pour the remaining oil mixture on top of the dhokra mixture.

7. Bake in a preheated oven at gas mark 2 (300°F or 150°C) for about 2½ hours on the middle shelf of the oven.

8. Leave the handva to cool for a few minutes and then cut into small pieces for serving. The cut pieces can be stored in a fridge, and warmed when needed for about 20 minutes, in a preheated oven before serving.

SAVOURY PEANUTS

Indians like spices in most of their snacks, and peanuts are no exception. They are usually served at parties, or with a glass of wine or a cup of tea. Savoury peanuts can be stored in an airtight tin for up to 3 weeks, and used as and when needed. For this recipe you need a wok or deep frying pan.

Ingredients   *Makes about 2 lb (900g) peanuts*

20 fl oz (600ml) cooking oil
2 lb (900g) peanuts

1 tsp salt
1 tsp chilli powder
1 tsp black pepper powder

Method   *Preparation and cooking time: 20 mins.*

1. Heat the oil to a high temperature, in a wok or deep frying pan. Once the oil is hot, reduce the heat and add a handful of peanuts. Deep fry until they are golden brown. This will usually take about 10 to 15 seconds. Remove the peanuts with a sieve and spread them on kitchen roll paper.

2. Repeat this with all the peanuts.

3. In a large mixing bowl, mix well the peanuts, salt, chilli powder and pepper powder.

4. Let the peanuts cool, and then transfer the contents to an airtight tin. They can be stored this way for up to 3 weeks.

SAVOURY CASHEW NUTS

Savoury cashew nuts taste excellent and are well worth a try. Like peanuts, they are usually served at parties, or with a glass of wine or a cup of tea. They can be stored in an airtight tin for up to 2 weeks, and used as and when needed. For this recipe you need a wok or deep frying pan.

Ingredients   *Makes about 2 lb (900g) cashew nuts*
20 fl oz (600ml) cooking oil
2 lb (900g) cashew nuts
1 tsp salt
1 tsp chilli powder
1 tsp black pepper powder

Method   *Preparation and cooking time: 20 mins.*

1. Heat the oil to a high temperature, in a wok or a deep

frying pan. Once the oil is hot, reduce the heat and add a handful of cashew nuts. Deep fry until they are golden brown. This will usually take about 10 to 15 seconds. Remove the cashew nuts with a sieve and spread them on kitchen roll paper.

2. Repeat this with all the cashew nuts.

3. In a large mixing bowl, mix the cashew nuts, salt, chilli powder and pepper powder well together.

4. Let the cashew nuts cool, and then transfer the contents to an airtight tin. They can be stored this way for up to 2 weeks.

POPPADUMS

Poppadums come in three main varieties – made from rice flour, moong dhal flour or urad dhal flour. Within these three varieties there are a number of sub-varieties, each having different quantities of spices mixed in them. When you buy poppadums, do check on whether they are hot or mild. It may be an idea to try different types to find out which you prefer. It is very difficult to recommend one particular variety, as it very much depends on individual taste.

Poppadums can be deep fried (one at a time, in about 40 fluid ounces (1 litre) of cooking oil heated to a high temperature), or grilled, like toast. It takes about half a minute to grill each side, but the deep fry method is much quicker, taking literally seconds, once the oil is heated.

It is normally recommended that rice poppadums should be deep fried, but dhal poppadums taste good done either way. In most restaurants, only fried poppadums are served.

3 MEAT, FISH AND EGG CURRIES

RED CHORI and MINCE CURRY
(Mince with red lentil-type seeds)

If you do not like beans but would like to try something similar to chilli con carne, then this is the dish for you. This mince curry is usually served with rice or chapattis. It can also be served with chips. For this recipe you need a liquidiser.

N.B. The chori must be boiled for about 45 minutes as indicated in the recipe otherwise it could cause indigestion.

Ingredients   *Serves 4*
2 oz (55g) red chori
15 fl oz (450ml) water for boiling red chori

(continued overleaf)

(contd from p. 59)
½ oz (10g) fresh garlic (peeled)
1 oz (25g) fresh ginger (peeled)
2 green chillies
1 fl oz (30ml) cooking oil
1 large onion, finely chopped
1 tsp tomato purée
½ tsp turmeric powder
½ tsp chilli powder
½ tsp tandoori masala
1 tsp garam masala
½ tsp salt
4 tsp soy sauce
8 oz (225g) minced beef
10 fl oz (300ml) water for cooking
Small amount green dhanyia (coriander), chopped

Method   Preparation and cooking time: 10 hrs. 30 mins.

1. Wash the red chori, like all dhals, and leave to soak in about 20 fluid ounces (600ml) of cold water for about 8 hours. (See page 16 on how to wash dhals.)

2. Strain the chori and put in a pan. Add the 15 fluid ounces of water. Place the pan on a hot ring, and bring the water to the boil. When the water has started to boil, cover the pan, lower the heat and simmer for a further 45 minutes.

3. Place garlic, ginger and green chillies into a liquidiser and chop very finely.

4. Heat the cooking oil in a large pan to a high temperature. Add the onion and cook until it is golden brown.

5. Add the contents of the liquidiser, tomato purée, turmeric powder, chilli powder, tandoori masala, garam

masala, salt and soy sauce. Cook this mixture for about 2 minutes.

6. Now add the boiled chori and the mince. Simmer gently for another 15 minutes stirring every 5 minutes.

7. Add the 10 fluid ounces of water, cover the pan and let it simmer for a further 45 minutes. Stir every 5 minutes.

8. Transfer the curry into a serving dish and garnish with fresh coriander. Serve while hot.

MINCED LAMB CURRY

This is a dry curry usually served with chapattis or pitta bread. It also makes excellent filling for toasted sandwiches. Bay leaves may be added to give the curry a nice fragrance and a slightly sharper taste. For this recipe you need a liquidiser.

Ingredients   *Serves 4*

½ oz (10g) fresh garlic (peeled)
1 oz (25g) fresh ginger (peeled)
3 green chillies
2 fl oz (60ml) cooking oil
1 large onion, finely chopped
2 tsp tomato purée
1 tsp turmeric powder
1 tsp chilli powder
2 tsp tandoori masala
1 tsp garam masala
1 tsp salt
2 bay leaves (optional)
12 oz (340g) of minced lamb
20 fl oz (600ml) water
Small amount green dhanyia (coriander) chopped

Method   *Preparation and cooking time: 50 mins.*

1. Place the garlic, ginger, and green chillies into a liquidiser and chop finely.

2. Heat the oil in a pan and add the chopped onion. Cook the onion until it is golden brown. Now add the liquidiser contents, tomato purée, turmeric powder, chilli powder, tandoori masala, garam masala, salt (and bay leaves if used). Cook for a further 5 minutes, stirring continuously.

3. Add the mince, and cook for a further 5 minutes, stirring continuously.

4. Add the water, cover the pan, reduce the heat and simmer gently for a further 30 minutes, stirring every 5 to 7 minutes.

5. Transfer the contents to a serving dish and garnish with fresh green coriander. Serve while hot.

6. The bay leaves (if used) are discarded while eating and left on the plate.

LAMB'S LIVER CURRY

This liver curry is usually eaten on its own, or served with chapattis or bread but is not served with rice. It is normally very mild but green fresh chillies can be added to make it slightly hot. For this recipe you need a liquidiser.

Ingredients   *Serves 4*

½ oz (10g) fresh garlic (peeled)
1 oz (25g) fresh ginger (peeled)
3 green chillies (optional for hot curry)
2 oz (55g) of tinned tomatoes
1 fl oz (30ml) cooking oil
1 large onion, finely chopped
1 lb (450g) lamb's liver, cut into small pieces
½ tsp turmeric powder

1 tsp tomato purée
½ tsp chilli powder
1 tsp tandoori masala
1 tsp salt
½ tsp garam masala
10 fl oz (300ml) of water
Small amount green dhanyia (coriander), chopped

Method   *Preparation and cooking time: 1 hr. 10 mins.*

1. Preheat the oven to mark 5 (375°F or 190°C). Place the garlic, ginger, green chillies (if used), and tomatoes in a liquidiser and blend them into a thick paste.

2. Place the oil in a pan. When hot, add the chopped onion. Cook the onion until it is golden brown. Add the contents of the liquidiser, liver pieces, turmeric powder, tomato purée, chilli powder, tandoori masala, salt and garam masala. Cook for about 10 minutes, stirring constantly. Place the curry in a casserole. Add water and stir.

3. Cover the casserole, and cook on the middle shelf of the preheated oven for about 45 to 50 minutes.

4. Garnish with green dhanyia (coriander) and serve while hot.

DRY BHOONA LAMB CHOPS

This is a very dry and mild curry which can be served with fried rice, or even mashed potatoes or chips. For this recipe you need a wok or deep frying pan.

Ingredients   *Serves 4*

8 lamb chops
3 fl oz (90ml) cooking oil
½ tsp whole jeera (cumin seeds)

(continued overleaf)

(contd from p. 63)

½ tsp whole rai (black mustard seeds)
8 oz (225g) onions, finely chopped
2 green chillies, finely chopped
4 oz (110g) tinned tomatoes, finely chopped
1½ tsp salt
1 tsp turmeric powder
1½ tsp garam masala
½ tsp chilli powder
4 fl oz (120ml) water
Small amount green dhania (coriander), chopped

Method   *Preparation and cooking time: 1 hr.*

1. Cut the fat from the lamb chops.

2. In a wok, or deep frying pan, heat the oil to a high temperature. Add the jeera and rai and let it cook for a few seconds. Add the chopped onions and the green chillies. Stir continuously and cook until the onions are golden brown. Add the tomatoes and cook for about a minute. Add the salt, turmeric powder, garam masala and chilli powder. Cook this spicy mixture for about another minute.

3. Add the lamb chops. Mix well, cover the pan, lower the heat and let it simmer for about 10 minutes, stirring every 3 to 4 minutes.

4. Add the water, mix well and simmer for another 40 minutes stirring every 8 to 10 minutes.

5. Transfer the contents to a serving dish and garnish with the green dhanyia (coriander).

SPINACH LAMB

Spinach is frequently used in Indian dishes, and spinach and lamb do make an excellent combination. This dish is quite mild, and can be served with chapattis, pitta bread, parothas or even bread. For this recipe you need a meat cleaver, or get your butcher to chop a leg of lamb up for you.

Ingredients   *Serves 4*

1½ lb (670g) leg of lamb
12 oz (340g) spinach
2 fl oz (60ml) cooking oil
1 large onion, finely chopped
3 tsp tomato purée
1 tsp salt
1 tsp turmeric powder
½ tsp chilli powder
1 tsp garam masala
4 fl oz (120ml) water

Method   *Preparation and cooking time: 1 hr. 10 mins.*

1. Chop the leg of lamb into small pieces, about 1 inch (2.5cm) in length. There is no need to remove the bones.

2. Cut the spinach into small pieces and wash well.

3. Heat the oil to a high temperature in a large pan. Add the onion and cook until the onion is golden brown. Add tomato purée, salt, turmeric powder, chilli powder and garam masala. Stir well and let the mixture cook for about 1 minute.

4. Add the lamb, spinach and the water. Mix well, lower the heat and simmer gently for about 40 minutes stirring every 5 to 7 minutes.

5. Transfer the contents to a serving dish and serve hot.

6. While eating, the bones are discarded and left on the plate.

LAMB VINDALOO

(Hot lamb and potato curry)

This is a very hot curry usually served with rice, chapattis or parothas.

Ingredients   *Serves 4*

1 lb (450g) potatoes
2 fl oz (60ml) cooking oil
1 large onion, finely chopped
6 green chillies, finely chopped
3 tsp tomato purée
2 tsp turmeric powder
2 tsp chilli powder
1 tsp garlic powder
1 tsp ginger powder
2 tsp salt
2 tsp garam masala
1 lb (450g) diced lamb
15 fl oz (450ml) water
Small amount green dhanyia (coriander), chopped

Method   *Preparation and cooking time: 1 hr.*

1. Peel the potatoes and cut into largish pieces (about 1 inch/2.5cm cubes).

2. Heat the oil to a high temperature in a large pan. Add the onion and chillies, and cook, stirring continuously, until the onion is golden brown.

3. Add the tomato purée, turmeric powder, chilli powder, garlic powder, ginger powder, salt, garam masala and the diced lamb. Mix well, lower the heat and simmer gently for about 5 minutes stirring ever 2 to 3 minutes.

4. Add the water and let the lamb simmer for about 35 minutes, stirring every 5 to 7 minutes.

5. Add the potatoes and simmer for another 20 minutes, stirring every 5 to 7 minutes.

6. Transfer the contents to a serving dish and garnish with green dhanyia (coriander).

CHICKEN VINDALOO
(Hot chicken and potato curry)

This is a very hot curry usually served with rice, chapattis or parothas. For this recipe you need a liquidiser and a chopper.

Ingredients   *Serves 4*

1 lb (450g) potatoes
2 lb (900g) fresh chicken
1 large onion
6 green chillies
½ oz (10g) fresh ginger
½ oz (10g) fresh garlic
2 fl oz (60ml) cooking oil
3 tsp tomato purée
2 tsp turmeric powder
2 tsp chilli powder
1 tsp garlic powder
1 tsp ginger powder
2 tsp salt
2 tsp garam masala
2 tsp tandoori powder
5 fl oz (150ml) water
Small amount green dhanyia (coriander), chopped

Method   *Preparation and cooking time: 50 mins.*

1. Peel the potatoes and cut into largish pieces (about 1 inch/2.5cm cubes).

2. Remove the skin from the chicken pieces and chop the chicken into small (about 3 inch (8cm) long) pieces.

3. Place the onion, chillies, ginger and garlic in a liquidiser and process until finely chopped.

4. Heat the oil to a high temperature in a large pan. Add the processed onions, chillies, ginger and garlic and cook, stirring continuously, until the onion is golden brown.

5. Add the tomato purée, turmeric powder, chilli powder, garlic powder, ginger powder, salt, garam masala, tandoori powder and the chicken. Mix well, lower the heat and simmer gently for about 10 minutes stirring every 2 to 3 minutes.

6. Add the water and let the chicken simmer for about 20 minutes, stirring every 5 to 7 minutes.

7. Add the potatoes and simmer for another 20 minutes, stirring every 5 to 7 minutes.

8. Transfer the contents to a serving dish and garnish with green dhanyia (coriander).

9. The bones are discarded while eating and left on the plate.

BEEF KOFTAS

(Beef meatballs)

Beef koftas are particularly good if you like mince dishes. They can be served with rice or chapattis. They can also be served with 'English side dishes' such as boiled potatoes, cabbage or cauliflower. For this recipe you need a liquidiser.

Ingredients   *Serves 4*

1 oz (25g) fresh garlic (peeled)
1 oz (25g) fresh ginger (peeled)

3 green chillies
1 lb (450 g) minced beef
1 tsp salt
½ tsp chilli powder
2 tsp tandoori masala
1 tsp garam masala
2 tsp tomato purée
Small amount green dhanyia (coriander), chopped
1 fl oz (30ml) cooking oil
2 medium sized onions, finely chopped
2 oz (55g) plum peeled tomatoes
10 fl oz (300ml) water

Method   *Preparation and cooking time: 1 hr. 50 mins.*

1. Place the garlic, ginger and green chillies into a liquidiser and process until finely chopped.

2. Mix the contents of the liquidiser with the mince, salt, chilli powder, tandoori masala, garam masala, tomato purée and fresh dhanyia and mix well. Shape the mixture into small meatballs approximately 2 inches (5cm) in diameter, and place them on a tray. Cover the tray.

3. Heat the oil in a large cooking pan. Add the onions and fry until they are golden brown. Now add the tomatoes and cook for a further 2 minutes.

4. Gently place 6 to 8 meatballs in the pan. Cover the pan, lower the heat and simmer for about 20 minutes. The meatballs will shrink in size and become golden brown. Carefully remove these balls from the onion and tomato mixture and place them on one side. Add another 6 to 8 fresh mince balls to the onion and tomato mixture, cover and simmer again for about the same period. Repeat this process until all the meatballs are done.

5. Now add all the meatballs to the onion and tomato mixture. Stir very gently and simmer for a further 50

minutes. Add the water, bring it to the boil, and simmer for a further 45 minutes, stirring every 10 minutes.

6. Transfer the contents to a serving dish and serve while hot.

BEEF CURRY

This is a hot curry. It can be eaten on its own, but is usually served with boiled noodles, rice, chapattis, bread, puris, parothas, mashed potatoes, or pitta bread. For this recipe you need a liquidiser.

Ingredients   *Serves 4*

1 lb (450g) shin or stewing beef
½ oz (10g) fresh garlic (peeled)
½ oz (10g) fresh ginger (peeled)
2 green chillies
2 oz (55g) plum peeled tomatoes
1 fl oz (30ml) cooking oil
1 large onion, finely chopped
½ tsp turmeric powder
1 tsp tomato purée
½ tsp chilli powder
1 tsp garam masala
1 tsp salt
1 tsp tandoori masala
4 tsp soy sauce
20 fl oz (600ml) of water
Small amount green dhanyia (coriander), chopped

Method   *Preparation and cooking time: 1 hr. 40 mins.*

1. Cut the beef into about 1 inch (2.5cm) cubes.

2. Place the garlic, ginger, green chillies, and tomatoes into a liquidiser, and blend them into a thick paste.

3. Heat the oil in a pan to a high temperature. Add the chopped onion and cook until it is golden brown. Add the beef cubes, blended paste, turmeric powder, tomato purée, chilli powder, garam masala, salt, tandoori masala, and soy sauce. Stir continuously for about 2 minutes. Reduce the heat, cover the pan and let it cook for about 20 minutes, stirring every few minutes. Add the water and stir. Simmer gently for a further hour.

4. Transfer the curry into a serving dish, and garnish with the fresh dhanyia (coriander).

MADRAS BUTTER BHOONA BEEF CURRY

This is a medium dry beef curry, usually served with rice or chapattis.

Ingredients   *Serves 4*

1 lb (450g) stewing beef
1 oz (25g) butter
1 large onion, finely chopped
2 oz (55g) plum peeled tomatoes, finely chopped
1 tsp tomato purée
1 tsp salt
1 tsp turmeric powder
1 tsp chilli powder
2 tsp madras curry powder
1 tsp garlic powder
15 fl oz (450ml) water
Small amount green dhanyia (coriander), chopped

Method   *Preparation and cooking time: 1 hr. 20 mins.*

1. Cut the beef into 1 inch (2½cm) cubes.

2. Melt the butter in a large pan; add the onion and cook

until golden brown, stirring continuously.

3. Add tomatoes, tomato purée, salt, turmeric powder, chilli powder, madras curry powder, garlic powder and the cubes of beef, and mix well. Stir continuously and cook for about 5 minutes.

4. Add the water, reduce the heat and simmer for about 1 hour stirring every 8 to 10 minutes.

5. Transfer the contents to a serving dish and garnish with the dhanyia (coriander).

FROZEN CHICKEN CURRY

This is a mild to medium hot chicken curry. It is usually served with a rice dish, or chapattis. You can either use fresh green chillies (if you like curry dishes hot) or a fresh green pepper for milder taste. Parsley or coriander can be used for garnishing. For this recipe you need a liquidiser.

Ingredients   *Serves 4*

2 lb (900g) frozen chicken pieces (thawed)
1 oz (25g) fresh garlic (peeled)
1 oz (25g) fresh ginger (peeled)
3 green chillies or 1 green pepper, chopped (dependent on taste)
2 fl oz (60ml) cooking oil
3 large onions, finely chopped
1 tsp turmeric powder
1 tsp chilli powder
2 tsp garam masala
1 tsp tandoori masala
3 tsp tomato purée
6 oz (170g) plum peeled tomatoes
2 tsp salt
Parsley or green fresh dhanyia (coriander)

Method   *Preparation and cooking time: 1 hr. 20 mins.*

1. Remove the skin from the chicken pieces.

2. Place the garlic, ginger and green chillies (or green pepper) in a liquidiser and process until finely chopped.

3. Heat the oil to a high temperature in a pan. Add the chopped onions and cook until they are golden brown. Add the chicken pieces, the contents of the liquidiser, turmeric powder, chilli powder, garam masala, tandoori masala, tomato purée, tomatoes and salt. Stir continuously for a few minutes.

4. Reduce the heat and simmer for about 1 hour stirring every 5 to 7 minutes, keeping the pan covered all the time.

5. Garnish with chopped parsley or fresh dhanyia (coriander).

6. The bones are discarded while eating and left on the plate.

FRESH CHICKEN CURRY

This is a very popular curry, usually served with rice or chapattis. It takes longer to cook than the frozen chicken curry, and tastes quite different.

Ingredients   *Serves 4*

2 fl oz (60ml) cooking oil
2 large onions, finely chopped
2 lb (900g) fresh chicken (skinned and cut into small pieces)
8 oz (225g) plum peeled tomatoes
1 tsp salt
1 tsp chilli powder
1 tsp turmeric powder
2 tsp garam masala
1 tsp garlic powder

(continued overleaf)

(contd from p. 73)

1 tsp ginger powder
3 green chillies (finely chopped)
20 fl oz (600ml) water
Small amount green dhanyia (coriander), chopped

Method   *Preparation and cooking time: 1 hr. 50 mins.*

1. Heat the oil in a large pan to a high temperature. Add the onions and cook until they are golden brown.

2. Add the chicken, tomatoes, salt, chilli powder, turmeric powder, garam masala, garlic powder, ginger powder and the green chillies. Stir continuously for about 5 minutes.

3. Cover the pan, reduce the heat and simmer gently for about 25 minutes.

4. Add half of the water (10 fluid ounces) to the curry and bring the mixture to the boil. Reduce the heat, cover the pan, and cook for a further 35 minutes, stirring every 10 minutes. Add the remaining water, and simmer for a further 45 minutes stirring every 15 minutes.

5. Transfer the contents to a serving dish, and garnish with the dhanyia (coriander). Serve while hot.

6. The bones are discarded while eating and left on the plate.

FRIED CHICKEN CURRY

This is a mouth-watering chicken curry, and is fairly simple to cook. It is usually served with chapattis, rice, noodles or even with chips or mashed potatoes. For this recipe you need either a meat cleaver or a very sharp knife, and a wok or deep frying pan.

Ingredients   *Serves 4*

2 lb (900g) chicken pieces
20 fl oz (600ml) cooking oil (for deep frying)
2 fl oz (60ml) cooking oil
3 large onions, finely chopped
1 tsp chilli powder
1 tsp garam masala
6 green chillies (finely chopped)
1 tsp garlic powder
2 tsp tandoori masala
1 tsp turmeric powder
1 tsp salt
4 tsp soy sauce
2 tsp tomato purée
10 fl oz (300ml) water
Small amount green dhanyia (coriander), chopped

Method   *Preparation and cooking time: 1 hr. 20 mins.*

1. Remove the skin from the chicken pieces, and chop the chicken into smaller pieces, about 3 inches (7cm) long. The bones are left in the chicken pieces.

2. Heat the 20 fluid ounces of cooking oil in a wok or deep frying pan to a high temperature. Deep fry all the chicken pieces, about 4 to 5 at a time, until they are golden brown.

3. Heat the 2 fluid ounces of oil in another pan and fry the chopped onions until they are golden brown. Add chilli powder, garam masala, green chillies, garlic powder, tandoori masala, turmeric powder, salt, soy sauce, and tomato purée. Mix well and cook for about 1 to 2 minutes.

4. Add the fried chicken, mix well and cook for a further 2 to 3 minutes stirring continuously. Add the water, stir, and bring the mixture to the boil. Reduce the heat; cover the pan and simmer gently for a further 15 minutes.

5. Transfer the curry to a serving dish and garnish with the

green dhanyia (coriander).

6. The bones are discarded while eating and left on the plate.

PORK CURRY

This is a dry hot curry. It can be eaten as a snack on its own, or served with mashed potatoes, chapattis, pitta bread or parothas. For this recipe you need a liquidiser.

Ingredients   *Serves 4*

2 lb (900g) boneless pork
½ oz (10g) fresh garlic (peeled)
½ oz (10g) fresh ginger (peeled)
2 green chillies
8 oz (225g) fresh tomatoes
1 fl oz (30ml) cooking oil
1 large onion, finely chopped
½ tsp turmeric powder
½ tsp chilli powder
½ tsp tandoori masala
1 tsp salt
1 tsp garam masala
4 fl oz (120ml) water
Small amount green dhanyia (coriander), chopped

Method   *Preparation and cooking time: 1 hr. 10 mins.*

1. Cut the pork pieces into about 1 inch (2.5cm) cubes.

2. Blend the garlic, ginger and green chillies in a liquidiser until finely chopped.

3. Cut the tomatoes into small pieces.

4. Heat the oil in a pan to a high temperature; add the chopped onion and cook until it is golden brown.

5. Add the contents of the liquidiser, tomatoes, pork

cubes, turmeric powder, chilli powder, tandoori masala, salt and garam masala. Stir continuously for about 2 minutes.

6. Reduce the heat, cover the pan and simmer gently for about 20 minutes stirring every 5 to 7 minutes.

7. Add the water, stir and simmer gently for a further 30 minutes, again stirring every 5 to 7 minutes.

8. Transfer the curry to a serving dish. Garnish with fresh green dhanyia (coriander) and serve while hot.

STUFFED MACKEREL CURRY

Spiced and stuffed mackerel is tasty and makes a good change from meat curries. It is usually served with fried rice and can be served with salad as a starter. For this recipe you need a liquidiser.

Ingredients   *Serves 4*

1 oz (25g) fresh garlic (peeled)
1 oz (25g) fresh ginger (peeled)
6 green chillies
2 tsp tomato purée
1 fl oz (30ml) yoghurt
½ tsp salt
½ tsp turmeric powder
½ tsp dhanyia powder (coriander)
½ tsp jeera powder (cumin)
1 tsp lemon juice
4 small fresh mackerel (about 1 lb in total (450g))
2 fl oz (60ml) cooking oil
Small amount green dhanyia (coriander), chopped

Method   *Preparation and cooking time: 8 hrs. 30 mins.*

1. Place the garlic, ginger, chillies, tomato purée, yoghurt,

salt, turmeric powder, dhanyia powder, jeera powder, and lemon juice in a liquidiser and blend into a thickish paste.

2. Cut the heads off the mackerel and slice the fish along their tops, on one side only, so as to enable you to remove the bones from their centres. Make sure that you do not cut completely through, and the mackerel are still whole.

3. Place the mackerel under cold running water for about one minute.

4. Carefully lay the four mackerel out in a large pan and pour the thick paste in the space left by the bones of each of the mackerel. Lift the other half and fold it back so that the blended liquid is in the middle of each of the mackerel.

5. Now leave the fish for about 8 hours.

6. Heat the oil to a high temperature, in a large flat pan. Transfer the fish very carefully to this pan with the hot oil, lower the heat and let it simmer for about 5 minutes. While simmering cover the pan. Turn the fish over carefully, still folded, and cook the other sides by simmering for a further 5 minutes.

7. Transfer the contents to a serving dish and garnish with the dhanyia (coriander). Serve while hot.

COD FISH CURRY

Cod curry is unusual but makes an excellent alternative to meat curries. It can be served with mashed potatoes, chapattis or fried rice. For this recipe you need a liquidiser.

Ingredients   *Serves 4*

½ oz (10g) fresh garlic (peeled)
½ oz (10g) fresh ginger (peeled)

1 green chilli
8 oz (225g) plum peeled tomatoes
2 fl oz (60ml) cooking oil
1 large onion, finely chopped
½ tsp turmeric powder
½ tsp chilli powder
½ tsp garam masala
½ tsp salt
1½ lb (670g) cod steaks
Small amount green dhanyia (coriander), chopped

Method   *Preparation and cooking time: 40 mins.*

1. Blend the garlic, ginger, chilli and tomatoes in a liquidiser, to a thickish paste.

2. Heat the oil to a high temperature in a pan; add the onion and cook until it is golden brown.

3. Add the contents of the liquidiser, turmeric powder, chilli powder, garam masala and salt, and stir continuously for about 2 minutes. Cook this mixture for a further 3 minutes.

4. Arrange the fish steaks in a large casserole and spread the spiced mixture on top of the steaks.

5. Bake the fish and the mixture in a pre-heated oven at mark 4 (350°F or 177°C), for about 20 minutes.

6. Garnish the fish with fresh green dhanyia (coriander) and serve hot.

PRAWN AND PEPPER CURRY

Prawns are rare in Indian homes, but prawn curries do taste good, and are always worth a try. For this recipe you need a deep frying pan or wok.

Ingredients   *Serves 4*

12 oz (340g) green peppers
2 fl oz (60ml) cooking oil
2 medium size onions, finely chopped
2 ripe tomatoes cut into small pieces
1 tsp salt
½ tsp turmeric powder
½ tsp chilli powder
½ tsp garam masala
12 oz (340g) peeled prawns

Method   *Preparation and cooking time: 25 mins.*

1. Chop the peppers lengthways into pieces about 1 inch (2.5cm) long and ½ inch (1cm) wide.

2. Heat the oil in a large wok, add the onions and fry them until they are golden brown. Add the tomatoes, salt, turmeric powder, chilli powder and garam masala. Cook for a further 2 minutes.

3. Add the peppers and prawns and stir well. Reduce the heat, cover the wok and cook on a very low heat for a further 15 minutes, stirring every 3 to 4 minutes.

4. Transfer the contents to a serving dish and serve hot.

DRY BHOONA MUSHROOM AND PRAWN CURRY

This is a very mild prawn curry usually served as a side dish with meat curry. For this recipe you need a liquidiser.

Ingredients   *Serves 4*

½ oz (10g) fresh garlic
½ oz (10g) fresh ginger
4 green chillies

2 fl oz (60ml) cooking oil
1 large onion, finely chopped
1 tsp tomato purée
½ tsp salt
½ tsp turmeric powder
½ tsp chilli powder
½ tsp dhanyia powder (coriander)
½ tsp jeera powder (cumin)
8 oz (225g) mushrooms, cut into halves
4 oz (110g) peeled prawns
Small amount green dhanyia (coriander), chopped
2 oz (55g) fresh tomatoes, cut into rings

Method   *Preparation and cooking time: 20 mins.*

1. Place the garlic, ginger and green chillies in a liquidiser, and chop finely.

2. Heat the oil to a high temperature, in a pan. Add the onion, stir continuously and cook until golden brown. Add the contents of the liquidiser, tomato purée, salt, turmeric powder, chilli powder, dhanyia powder and jeera powder. Cook the mixture for a further minute, stirring continuously.

3. Add the mushrooms and prawns. Mix well, lower the heat, cover the pan and simmer gently for about 8 minutes, stirring every 2 to 3 minutes.

4. Transfer the contents to a serving dish and garnish with the green dhanyia and tomatoes.

EGG AND POTATO CURRY

This is a mild curry not usually served in restaurants. It can be served with rice or chapattis.

Ingredients   *Serves 4*

6 eggs
8 oz (225g) potatoes
1 fl oz (30ml) cooking oil
1 onion, finely chopped
4 oz (110g) plum peeled tomatoes
1 tsp salt
1 tsp turmeric powder
1 tsp garam masala
½ tsp chilli powder
½ tsp tandoori masala
1 tsp cumin powder
5 fl oz (150ml) water
Small amount green dhanyia (coriander), chopped

Method   *Preparation and cooking time: 45 mins.*

1. Hard boil the eggs and remove the shells. Cut the eggs into halves.

2. Peel the potatoes and cut into small pieces, about ½ inch (1cm) cubes.

3. Heat the oil to a high temperature in a pan. Add the onion and cook until the onion is golden brown, stirring continuously.

4. Add the tomatoes and cook for about a further 2 minutes stirring continuously. Now add the salt, turmeric powder, garam masala, chilli powder, tandoori masala and cumin powder. Cook for a further 1 minute.

5. Add the potatoes, mix well, and cook for about 2 minutes stirring continuously. Now add the eggs and cook for about 3 to 4 minutes.

6. Add the water; bring it to the boil; lower the heat and let it simmer for about 20 minutes, stirring every 5 to 7 minutes.

7. Transfer the contents to a serving dish and garnish with the coriander.

4 DHALS

VALL DHALS

This is a dhal curry usually served with chapattis, bread, rice or pitta bread.

Ingredients   *Serves 4*

8 oz (225g) vall dhal
30 fl oz (900ml) water
1 fl oz (30ml) cooking oil
½ tsp whole jeera (cumin seeds)
½ tsp whole rai (black mustard seeds)
¼ tsp hing (asafoetida)
2 tsp tomato purée
1 tsp turmeric powder
1 tsp chilli powder
1 tsp garlic powder

(continued overleaf)

(contd from p. 83)

1 tsp ginger powder
1 tsp salt
1 tsp garam masala
Small amount green dhanyia (coriander), chopped

Method   *Preparation and cooking time: 2 hrs. 40 mins.*

1. Wash the vall dhal as described in the introduction (page 16). Then leave the dhal to soak in the 30 fluid ounces of water for 2 hours.

2. Heat the oil to a high temperature, in a pan. Add jeera to the hot oil, and then a few seconds later add the rai and asafoetida. Leave for a few more seconds and add tomato purée, turmeric powder, chilli powder, garlic powder, ginger powder, salt and garam masala. Cook for a further 2 minutes, stirring continuously.

3. Drain the dhal, and save the water in which it was soaking, in another pan. Add the dhal to the spiced mixture. Cook for a further 2 minutes stirring continuously.

4. Add the water in which the dhal was soaked to the above mixture. Bring the water to the boil and simmer gently for a further 30 minutes, stirring every 5 minutes.

5. Place the dhal in a serving dish and garnish with fresh dhanyia (coriander).

SPLIT URAD DHAL

This dhal curry is usually served with chapattis or bread. It can also be served with hot pitta bread. It is very popular with vegetarians. Green chillies can be used if you like hot curries, but otherwise a pepper can be used for a milder taste. For this recipe you need a liquidiser.

Ingredients   *Serves 4*

6 oz (170g) skinless split urad dhal
1 large onion, finely chopped
40 fl oz (1200ml) water
1 tsp salt
3 oz (85g) plum peeled tomatoes
3 green chillies or 1 green pepper, chopped
1 oz (25g) fresh garlic (peeled)
1 oz (25g) fresh ginger (peeled)
2 fl oz (60ml) cooking oil
½ tsp whole jeera (cumin seeds)
½ tsp whole rai (black mustard seeds)
1 tsp turmeric powder
1 tsp chilli powder
1 tsp garam masala
Small amount green dhanyia (coriander), chopped

Method   *Preparation and cooking time: 1 hr. 25 mins.*

1. Wash the dhal as described in the introduction.

2. Place the washed dhal, chopped onion and the 40 fluid ounces of water in a large pan.

3. Add the salt.

4. Bring the water to the boil, reduce the heat, and simmer gently for about 1 hour, stirring every 5 to 7 minutes.

5. Place the tomatoes, green chillies, garlic and ginger in a liquidiser and blend into a thickish paste.

6. Heat the oil to a high temperature, in a separate pan. Add jeera and rai and let it cook for a few seconds. Add the contents of the liquidiser, turmeric powder, chilli powder and garam masala. Stir continuously and cook for 2 to 3 minutes.

7. Add this spicy mixture to the boiled dhal, and boil for

another 5 minutes.

8. Place the dhal in a serving dish and garnish with fresh dhanyia (coriander).

RED KIDNEY BEANS (whole) DHAL

This is a very popular curry all over India. It is usually served with chapattis, bread, pitta bread, puris, parothas, or simply rice. If you like sweet and sour dishes then sugar can be added to give it a slightly sweeter taste. This makes it very versatile. For this recipe you need a liquidiser.

N.B. Red kidney beans must be boiled for at least 1 hour as indicated in this recipe, otherwise they could be poisonous.

Ingredients   *Serves 4*

6 oz (170g) red kidney beans
40 fl oz (1200ml) water
1 tsp salt
2 oz (55g) plum peeled tomatoes
2 green chillies
1 oz (25g) fresh garlic (peeled)
2 fl oz (60ml) cooking oil
½ tsp whole jeera (cumin seeds)
½ tsp whole rai (black mustard seeds)
1 large onion, finely chopped
1 tsp tandoori masala
1 tsp turmeric powder
1 tsp garam masala
1 tsp sugar (optional)
1 fl oz (30ml) lemon juice
1 tsp tomato purée
½ tsp chilli powder
Small amount green dhanyia (coriander), chopped

Method   *Preparation and cooking time: 2 hrs. 20 mins.*

1. Boil the beans in the 40 fluid ounces of salted water for about 1 hour and 15 minutes. This will make the beans soft, and this can be tested by being able to pulp the bean easily, with your fingers.

2. Place the tomatoes, green chillies, and garlic in a liquidiser, and blend to a thickish paste.

3. Heat the oil to a high temperature, in a large pan. Add the whole jeera and rai and cook for a few seconds. Add the onion and cook until it is golden brown.

4. Add the contents of the liquidiser, tandoori masala, turmeric powder, garam masala, sugar (if required), lemon juice, tomato purée and chilli powder. Cook together for a further 1 minute.

5. Add the beans with the water. Lower the heat, and simmer gently for a further 30 minutes, stirring every 5 to 7 minutes.

6. Transfer the contents to a serving dish and garnish with fresh dhanyia (coriander). Serve hot.

WHOLE URAD AND RED KIDNEY BEANS DHAL

This is a rather mild dhal. Like all dhals, it is usually served with boiled rice or chapattis but can be served with bread. If you like hot curries then green chillies should be used, but otherwise a green pepper can be used instead.

N.B. The urad and red kidney beans must be boiled for at least 2 hours as indicated in the recipe, otherwise the beans are poisonous.

Ingredients   *Serves 4*

3 oz (85g) whole urad
1 oz (25g) red kidney beans
60 fl oz (1800ml) water
1 large onion, finely chopped
2 green chillies, finely chopped, or 1 green pepper, finely
   chopped
1 tsp salt
1 fl oz (30ml) cooking oil
½ tsp whole jeera (cumin seeds)
2 tsp tomato purée
½ tsp turmeric powder
1 tsp chilli powder
1 tsp garam masala
Some fresh green dhanyia (coriander), finely chopped

Method   *Preparation and cooking time: 2 hrs. 40 mins.*

1. Mix the urad and red kidney beans. Wash the beans and urad as described in the introduction (page 16).

2. Place the washed, mixed dhal in the 60 fluid ounces of water.

3. Add the chopped onion, the chopped chillies (or green pepper), and the salt, and bring to the boil.

4. Reduce the heat, cover the pan and boil gently, stirring every 15 minutes until the consistency is like thin porridge. This usually takes about two and a half hours.

5. Heat the oil to a high temperature, in a separate pan. Add the jeera, tomato purée, turmeric powder, chilli powder, and garam masala. Stir continuously and simmer the mixture for about 1 minute. Add the mixture to the dhal and simmer the dhal gently for another 3 to 5 minutes.

6. Transfer the cooked dhal to a serving dish and garnish with the fresh dhanyia (coriander).

SPLIT MOONG AND SPLIT LENTIL DHAL

This is a mixed dhal, usually served with chapattis, bread, puris (deep fried chapattis – see recipe on page 142), parothas, rice or pitta bread. It can also be used like a soup, as a starter. It is very popular with vegetarians.

Ingredients   *Serves 4*

3 oz (85g) skinless, split moong dhal
3 oz (85g) skinless, split lentil dhal
30 fl oz (900ml) water
1 large onion, finely chopped
1 tsp salt
2 fl oz (60ml) cooking oil
½ tsp whole jeera (cumin seeds)
½ tsp whole rai (black mustard seeds)
2 tsp tomato purée
1 tsp turmeric powder
1 tsp garam masala
6 bay leaves
1 tsp chilli powder
Small amount green dhanyia (coriander), chopped

Method   *Preparation and cooking time: 45 mins.*

1. Mix the moong and lentil dhals. Wash the dhal as described in the introduction.

2. Place the washed dhal, the chopped onion and the 30 fluid ounces of water in a large pan and add the salt.

3. Bring the water to the boil, reduce the heat and simmer gently for about 30 minutes, stirring every 5 to 7 minutes.

4. Heat the oil to a high temperature, in a separate pan. Add jeera and rai and leave it to cook for a few seconds. Add the tomato purée, turmeric powder, garam masala, bay leaves and chilli powder. Stir continuously and cook

for a few seconds. Pour the boiled dhal into the mixture, and simmer for a further 5 minutes.

5. Transfer the dhal to a serving dish and garnish with fresh dhanyia (coriander).

6. The bay leaves are discarded and left on the plate, while eating.

WHOLE LENTIL DHAL

This is a rather mild dhal. It is usually served with boiled rice, chapattis or bread. Chilli powder can be used for making a hot dhal, otherwise paprika powder can be used for a milder taste. Fresh parsley or green fresh coriander can be used for garnishing.

Ingredients   *Serves 4*

6 oz (170g) whole lentils
30 fl oz (900ml) water
1½ tsp salt
2 fl oz (60ml) cooking oil
½ tsp whole jeera (cumin seeds)
1 large onion, finely chopped
2 tsp tomato purée
1 tsp turmeric powder
1 tsp chilli powder, or paprika powder for mild taste
2 tsp garam masala
1 tsp tandoori masala
Some fresh parsley or green fresh dhanyia (coriander),
    finely chopped

Method   *Preparation and cooking time: 55 mins.*

1. Wash the whole lentils, as described in the introduction (page 16).

2. Place the washed lentils in the 30 fluid ounces of water,

add the salt and bring to the boil.

3. Reduce the heat, cover the pan and simmer gently for about 45 minutes stirring every 5 to 7 minutes.

4. Heat the oil to a high temperature, in a separate pan. When it is hot, add the jeera and the chopped onion. Cook together until the onion is golden brown. Add tomato purée, turmeric powder, chilli powder (or paprika powder), garam masala and tandoori masala. Stir continuously and simmer the mixture for about 1 minute.

5. Add the spiced mixture to the cooked lentil dhal.

6. Simmer gently for about 3 to 5 minutes. Transfer the contents to a serving dish and garnish with the dhanyia or parsley.

SPLIT LENTIL DHAL

This dhal tastes very different from whole lentil and is usually served with plain boiled rice, or sometimes like soup, as a starter.

Ingredients   *Serves 4*

6 oz (170g) skinless split lentils
40 fl oz (1200ml) water
1 large onion, finely chopped
1 tsp salt
2 fl oz (60ml) cooking oil
½ tsp whole jeera (cumin seeds)
½ tsp whole rai (black mustard seeds)
2 oz (55g) plum peeled tomatoes
1 tsp turmeric powder
½ tsp garam masala
½ tsp chilli powder
Small amount green dhanyia (coriander), chopped

Method   *Preparation and cooking time: 40 mins.*

1. Wash the dhal as described in the introduction (page 16).

2. Place the dhal, the 40 fluid ounces of water and the chopped onion in a large pan. Add the salt and stir well.

3. Bring the water to the boil, reduce the heat and simmer gently for about 30 minutes, stirring every 5 to 7 minutes. This boiled dhal can be served as soup if desired.

4. Heat the oil to a high temperature, in a separate pan or wok. Add jeera and rai and leave it to cook for a few seconds. Add the tomatoes, turmeric powder, garam masala, and chilli powder. Stir continuously and cook until the tomatoes have reduced to a pulp. This will usually take about 2 to 3 minutes.

5. Add the boiled dhal to this spice mixture, reduce the heat and simmer gently for a further 5 minutes.

6. Transfer the contents to a serving dish and garnish with the fresh green dhanyia (coriander). Serve hot.

WHOLE MOONG, DRY

This is one of the many dhal curries usually served with chapattis. It also makes a good filling for toasted sandwiches. It may also be served with rice and a meat curry dish.

Ingredients   *Serves 4*

6 oz (170g) whole moong
40 fl oz (1200ml) water for soaking moong
2 fl oz (60ml) cooking oil
½ tsp whole jeera (cumin seeds)
½ tsp whole rai (black mustard seeds)
1 tsp turmeric powder
1 tsp garam masala

1 tsp chilli powder
2 tsp tomato purée
1 tsp salt
4 tsp soy sauce
15 fl oz (450ml) water for cooking
Small amount green dhanyia (coriander), chopped

Method   *Preparation and cooking time: 10 hrs. 30 mins.*

1. Soak the moong overnight in the 40 fluid ounces of water.

2. Wash the whole moong as described in the introduction.

3. Heat the oil to a high temperature, in a separate pan. Add jeera and rai, and leave it to cook for a few seconds. Add the washed moong, turmeric powder, garam masala, chilli powder, tomato purée, salt and soy sauce. Stir continuously and cook for about 3 minutes. Add the 15 fluid ounces of water and bring it to the boil.

4. Reduce the heat, cover the pan and simmer gently for about 30 minutes, stirring every 5 to 7 minutes.

5. Transfer the contents to a serving dish and garnish with fresh green dhanyia (coriander).

SPLIT MOONG DHAL

This is one of the many dhal curries usually served with chapattis, bread or rice. Like most dhals it is popular with vegetarians.

Ingredients   *Serves 4*
6 oz (170g) skinless split moong dhal
1 tsp salt
1 large onion, finely chopped

(continued overleaf)

(contd from p. 93)

30 fl oz (900ml) water
2 fl oz (60ml) cooking oil
½ tsp whole jeera (cumin seeds)
½ tsp whole rai (black mustard seeds)
1 oz (25g) fresh garlic (peeled), finely chopped
3 oz (85g) plum peeled tomatoes
1 tsp turmeric powder
1 tsp garam masala
1 tsp chilli powder
Small amount green dhanyia (coriander), chopped

Method   *Preparation and cooking time: 40 mins.*

1. Wash the dhal as described in the introduction.

2. Add the salt, chopped onion and the water to the washed dhal. Boil the water, lower the heat and simmer gently for about 30 minutes stirring every 5 to 7 minutes.

3. Heat the oil to a high temperature, in a separate pan and add jeera, rai and the chopped garlic. Cook for a few seconds. Add the tomatoes, turmeric powder, garam masala and chilli powder and cook for a further 3 to 4 minutes, stirring continuously.

4. Add this spice mixture to the boiled dhal, and simmer gently for a further 5 to 7 minutes.

5. Transfer the dhal to a serving dish and garnish with the fresh green dhanyia (coriander).

TOOVAR DHAL

This is one of the popular dhals of southern India, and has a sweet and sour taste. It is usually served with chapattis, bread, puris (deep fried chapattis – see recipe on page 142), parothas or rice. It is a dish which pleases vegetarians. For this recipe you need a pressure cooker.

Ingredients   *Serves 4*

6 oz (170g) toovar dhal
30 fl oz (900ml) water
1 tsp salt
2 fl oz (60ml) cooking oil
½ tsp whole jeera (cumin seeds)
½ tsp whole rai (black mustard seeds)
4 whole cloves
4 whole black peppercorns
¼ tsp hing (asafoetida)
1 tsp tomato purée
1 tsp turmeric powder
6 bay leaves
1 tsp chilli powder
2 green chillies, sliced into halves
½ tsp sugar
½ oz (10g) peanuts
½ fl oz (15ml) lemon juice
Small amount green dhanyia (coriander), chopped

Method   *Preparation and cooking time: 40 mins.*

1. Wash the dhal as described in the introduction.

2. Place the washed dhal in a pressure cooker, add the 30 fluid ounces of water and salt, and cook on high pressure for about 15 minutes after the initial boil whistle. Switch off the heat, but leave the dhal cooking in the pressure cooker.

3. Heat the oil to a high temperature in a separate pan and add jeera, rai, cloves, peppercorns, and asafoetida. Cook for a few seconds. Add the tomato purée, turmeric powder, bay leaves, chilli powder, green chillies, sugar, peanuts, and lemon juice. Stir continuously for a few seconds. Pour the boiled dhal into the mixture and simmer gently together for a further 10 minutes, stirring every 2

minutes.

4. Transfer the dhal into a serving dish and garnish with the dhanyia (coriander). Serve hot.

5. The bay leaves and peppercorns are discarded and left on the plate while eating.

BLACK CHANA DHAL

Black chana are more common in southern India than in the north, and taste somewhat like chick peas. They are not usually served in restaurants, and therefore are worth trying at home.

Ingredients   *Serves 4*

12 oz (340g) black chana
30 fl oz (900ml) water for soaking the chana
30 fl oz (900ml) water for boiling the chana
1 tsp salt
2 fl oz (60ml) cooking oil
½ tsp whole jeera (cumin seeds)
¼ tsp hing (asafoetida)
½ tsp whole rai (black mustard seeds)
2 tsp tomato purée
½ tsp chilli powder
1 tsp tandoori masala
½ tsp turmeric powder
4 green chillies, finely chopped
1 tsp garam masala
1 fl oz (30ml) lemon juice
15 fl oz (450ml) water for cooking
Small amount green dhanyia (coriander), chopped

Method   Preparation and cooking time: 11 hrs. 20 mins.

1. Wash the chana as described in the introduction.

2. Soak the chana overnight in the 30 fluid ounces of water.

3. Next day, drain the water. Add the fresh 30 fluid ounces of water and the salt and bring the mixture to the boil. Reduce the heat, cover the pan and simmer gently for about 1 hour.

4. Heat the oil to a high temperature, in a separate pan or wok. Add jeera, asafoetida, and the rai. Cook for a few seconds. Add tomato purée, chilli powder, tandoori masala, turmeric powder, green chillies, garam masala and lemon juice. Stir well and cook for a further few seconds.

5. Now add the chana and the 15 fluid ounces of water for cooking. Bring the water to the boil; lower the heat and then simmer gently for a further 15 minutes.

6. Transfer the contents to a serving dish and garnish with fresh green dhanyia (coriander).

WHITE CHANA DHAL

White chana curry is a traditional dish in the Punjab and northern parts of India. It is a very special dish for dinner parties, wedding parties, picnics etc. It is usually served with bhaturas, puris, chapattis, or even pitta bread. It also makes a good filling for toasted sandwiches.

Ingredients   *Serves 4*

12 oz (340g) white chana
30 fl oz (900ml) water for soaking chana
30 fl oz (900ml) water for boiling chana
1 tsp salt
2 fl oz (60ml) cooking oil
½ tsp whole jeera (cumin seeds)
½ tsp whole rai (black mustard seeds)

(continued overleaf)

(contd from p. 97)

2 large onions, finely chopped
3 green chillies, finely chopped
2 tsp tomato purée
½ tsp chilli powder
1½ tsp tandoori masala
1 tsp turmeric powder
½ tsp garlic powder
1½ tsp garam masala
1 fl oz (30ml) lemon juice

For garnishing
Small tomato, cut into round rings
1 onion, cut into small rings
Small amount green dhanyia (coriander), chopped

Method   Preparation and cooking time: 11 hrs. 40 mins.

1. Wash the chana as described in the introduction.

2. Soak the chana overnight in the 30 fluid ounces of water.

3. Next day, drain the water. Place the chana in a large cooking pot, add the fresh 30 fluid ounces water and the salt, and bring the mixture to the boil. Reduce the heat, cover the pan and simmer gently for about 1 hour.

4. In a separate pan, heat the oil to a high temperature. Add jeera and rai; cook for a few seconds until they are slightly brown. Add the onions and green chillies, and cook until the onions are golden brown. Add tomato purée, chilli powder, tandoori masala, turmeric powder, garlic powder, garam masala and lemon juice. Stir continuously and cook for a further 2 minutes.

5. Drain the chana, but save the water. Add the drained chana to the spice mixture. Cook for a further 2 minutes, stirring continuously. Add the water which was drained

from the chana, reduce the heat, cover the pan and simmer for about 5 minutes.

6. Place the cooked chana in a serving dish and garnish with tomatoes, onion and dhanyia. Serve while hot, or allow to cool and use as filling for toasted sandwiches.

BLACK EYE BEANS DHAL

Black eye beans taste similar to chick peas, and are usually served with rice.

N.B. The beans must be cooked for at least 20 minutes, otherwise they could cause indigestion.

Ingredients   *Serves 4*

8 oz (225g) black eye beans
30 fl oz (900ml) water for soaking
2 fl oz (60ml) cooking oil
½ tsp whole jeera (cumin seeds)
½ tsp whole rai (black mustard seeds)
1 tsp salt
1 tsp turmeric powder
1 tsp chilli powder
1 tsp dhanyia powder (coriander)
1 tsp jeera powder (cumin)
2 tsp tomato purée
20 fl oz (600ml) water for cooking
Small amount of dhanyia (coriander)

Method   *Preparation and cooking time: 11 hrs.*

1. Soak the beans overnight in the 30 fluid ounces of water.

2. Wash the beans as described in the introduction (page 16).

3. Heat the oil to a high temperature, in a large pan. Add the jeera and rai and let it cook for a few seconds. Add the washed beans, salt, turmeric powder, chilli powder, dhanyia powder, jeera powder and tomato purée. Mix well and cook for about 2 minutes stirring continuously.

4. Add the 20 fluid ounces of water, bring to the boil, lower the heat, cover the pan and simmer for about 25 minutes stirring every 5 to 7 minutes.

5. Transfer the contents to a serving dish and garnish with the dhanyia. Serve while hot.

CHANA AND MARROW DHAL

Dhals are sometimes cooked mixed with other dhals or vegetables. Marrow makes a very good addition to the chana dhal and is well worth a try. For this recipe you need a pressure cooker.

Ingredients   *Serves 4*

4 oz (110g) chana dhal
8 oz (225g) marrow, peeled and diced into small cubes
30 fl oz (900ml) water
1 tsp salt
2 fl oz (60ml) cooking oil
4 oz (110g) onions, finely chopped
3 oz (85g) tomatoes, finely chopped
1 tsp turmeric powder
1 tsp chilli powder
1 tsp garam masala
3 green chillies, finely chopped
2 tsp lemon juice
Small amount green dhanyia (coriander), chopped

Method   *Preparation and cooking time: 1 hr. 20 mins.*

1. Wash the dhal as described in the introduction (page 16).

2. Place the washed dhal and marrow in a pressure cooker. Add the water and salt, cover the lid and cook for about 30 minutes on high pressure. Switch off the heat after this time but leave the dhal cooking in the pressure cooker for another 30 minutes.

3. Heat the oil to a high temperature, in another pan. Add the onions and cook them until they are golden brown. Add the tomatoes, turmeric powder, chilli powder, garam masala, green chillies and the lemon juice. Cook this spice mixture for about another 2 minutes.

4. Add the spice mixture to the dhal, stir well and cook together for about 5 minutes stirring every 2 to 3 minutes.

5. Transfer the dhal to a serving dish and garnish with the dhanyia. Serve hot.

5 VEGETABLE CURRIES

FROZEN MIXED VEGETABLE CURRY

If you are in a hurry, then this curry is ideal. It does not take too long to cook, and can be served with plain boiled rice. It is also good served with bread, or chapattis.

Ingredients   *Serves 4*

1½ fl oz (45ml) cooking oil
½ tsp whole jeera (cumin seeds)
½ tsp whole rai (black mustard seeds)
1 large onion, finely chopped
2 tsp tomato purée
1 tsp turmeric powder
1 tsp chilli powder
1 tsp garam masala
1 tsp salt
1 tsp garlic powder
1 lb (450g) frozen, mixed vegetables

2 small potatoes, chopped into very small pieces
10 fl oz (300ml) water

Method   *Preparation and cooking time: 30 mins.*

1. Heat the oil to a high temperature in a pan, and add jeera, rai and chopped onion. Cook together until the onion is golden brown.

2. Add tomato purée, turmeric powder, chilli powder, garam masala, salt, garlic powder, mixed vegetables and potatoes. Stir continuously and cook for a further 5 minutes.

3. Add the water to the vegetables, and bring to the boil. Reduce the heat and simmer gently for about 20 minutes.

4. Serve hot.

CUT OKRA CURRY

Okra, also sometimes called ladies' fingers, is a very popular vegetable in India. Like most vegetable curries, this is usually served with dhal and rice, or meat curry and rice. It may also be served with chapattis alone. For this recipe you need a liquidiser.

Ingredients   *Serves 4*
1 oz (25g) fresh garlic (peeled)
2 green chillies
2 oz (55g) fresh ginger (peeled)
12 oz (340g) fresh okra
3 fl oz (90ml) cooking oil
12 oz (340g) onions, chopped into large pieces
2 tsp tomato purée
1 tsp salt
½ tsp chilli powder

(continued overleaf)

(contd from p. 103)

½ tsp turmeric powder
1 tsp garam masala
1 fresh tomato, cut into small pieces, for garnish

Method   *Preparation and cooking time: 45 mins.*

1. Place the garlic, green chillies, and ginger into a liquidiser and chop finely.

2. Wash the okra and then dry each piece individually with kitchen roll paper. This is very important as okra should be as dry as possible.

3. Cut the okra into ½ inch (1cm) long pieces, lengthways.

4. Heat the oil to a high temperature, in a pan, add the contents of the liquidiser, and cook for a few seconds. Add the onions and cook together, stirring continuously, until the onions are very light brown. Add the tomato purée, salt, chilli powder, turmeric powder, and garam masala. Cook for a few seconds, and add the okra. Stir continuously for 2 to 3 minutes.

5. Reduce the heat, cover the pan and simmer gently for about 25 minutes. The heat must be kept very low, and the mixture needs to be stirred every 5 to 7 minutes.

6. Transfer the okra curry into a serving dish and garnish with the fresh tomato pieces.

OKRA & CHIPS CURRY

Okra, or ladies' fingers, is a very popular vegetable in Indian homes, and since most people like potatoes, okra and chips make an attractive combination.

Ingredients   *Serves 4*

8 oz (225g) fresh okra
2 fl oz (60ml) cooking oil

3 large onions, finely chopped
½ tsp salt
½ tsp turmeric powder
½ tsp chilli powder
½ tsp garam masala
½ tsp tomato purée
4 oz (110g) fried potato chips
1 fresh tomato, cut into small pieces

Method   *Preparation and cooking time: 25 mins.*

1. Wash the okra and then dry each piece individually with kitchen roll paper. This is extremely important as okra must be as dry as possible.

2. Cut the okra into ½ inch (1cm) long pieces lengthways.

3. Heat the oil to a high temperature in a wok or deep frying pan. Add the onions and the okra. Stir, reduce the heat, cover the pan and let the okra and onions cook for about 10 minutes, stirring every 3 to 4 minutes.

4. Now add the salt, turmeric powder, chilli powder, garam masala and tomato purée. Mix well and let it cook for a further 3 to 4 minutes.

5. Add the chips, mix well and let it cook for another 3 to 4 minutes.

6. Transfer the contents to a serving dish and garnish with the tomato.

MADRAS POTATO AND PEA CURRY

This is one of the many vegetable dishes served with another main dish and rice.

Ingredients   *Serves 4*

12 oz (340g) potatoes
2 fl oz (60ml) cooking oil
½ tsp whole jeera (cumin seeds)
½ tsp whole rai (black mustard seeds)
2 large onions, finely chopped
6 oz (170g) frozen peas
½ tsp chilli powder
½ tsp turmeric powder
1 tsp madras curry powder
1 tsp salt
2 tsp tomato purée
10 fl oz (300ml) water
Small amount green dhanyia (coriander), chopped

Method   *Preparation and cooking time: 30 mins.*

1. Peel the potatoes and cut them into about 1 inch (2.5cm) cubes.

2. Heat the oil to a high temperature, in a large pan. Add jeera, rai and onions. Stir continuously and cook until the onions are golden brown. Add potatoes, peas, chilli powder, turmeric powder, madras curry powder, salt and tomato purée. Stir continuously for 2 minutes. Add the water and bring to the boil. Lower the heat and simmer gently for about 20 minutes.

3. Transfer the curry to a serving dish and garnish with fresh green dhanyia.

GUJARATI POTATO CURRY

This is a very popular curry in a part of India which is well known for its vegetable dishes. It is usually served with some other curry (such as dhal or meat) and rice.

Ingredients   *Serves 4*

1 lb (450g) potatoes
1 fl oz (30ml) cooking oil
½ tsp whole jeera (cumin seeds)
½ tsp whole rai (black mustard seeds)
¼ tsp hing (asafoetida)
½ tsp turmeric powder
½ tsp jeera powder (cumin powder)
½ tsp dhanyia powder (coriander powder)
1 tsp salt
1 tsp red chilli powder
2 oz (55g) tinned tomatoes or
**   2 tsp tomato purée**
15 fl oz (450ml) water
Small amount green dhanyia (coriander), chopped

Method   *Preparation and cooking time: 35 mins.*

1. Peel the potatoes and cut into about 1 inch (2.5cm) cubes.

2. Heat the oil to a high temperature in a large pan and add jeera, rai and asafoetida. Leave to cook for a few seconds. Add potatoes, turmeric powder, jeera powder, dhanyia powder, salt, chilli powder, and tomatoes (or purée). Stir continuously and cook for about 5 minutes.

3. Add the water and bring it to the boil. Lower the heat and simmer gently for about 20 minutes.

4. Place the curry in a serving dish and garnish with fresh dhanyia.

BOMBAY POTATO CURRY

This is a common curry in most Indian restaurants. It is very simple to cook and usually served with some other curry (such as dhal or meat) and rice.

Ingredients   *Serves 4*

1 lb (450g) potatoes
1 fl oz (30ml) cooking oil
1 tsp whole jeera (cumin seeds)
½ tsp whole rai (black mustard seeds)
½ tsp turmeric powder
1 tsp salt
½ tsp chilli powder
4 oz fresh tomatoes, finely chopped
5 fl oz (150ml) water
Small amount green dhanyia (coriander), chopped

Method   *Preparation and cooking time: 35 mins.*

1. Peel the potatoes and cut into 1 inch (2.5cm) cubes.

2. Heat the oil to a high temperature in a large pan and add jeera, and rai. Leave to cook for a few seconds. Add potatoes, turmeric powder, salt, chilli powder and tomatoes. Stir continuously and cook for about 5 minutes.

3. Add the water and bring to the boil. Lower the heat and simmer gently for about 20 minutes.

4. Place the curry in a serving dish and garnish with fresh dhanyia.

PUNJABI POTATO CURRY

This is a popular curry in northern parts of India. It is usually served with parothas or puris (deep fried chapattis – see recipe on page 142).

Ingredients   *Serves 4*

1 lb (450g) potatoes
1 oz (25g) butter
1 large onion, finely chopped

2 green chillies, finely chopped
1 tsp turmeric powder
1 tsp ginger powder
½ tsp dhanyia powder (coriander powder)
1 tsp salt
½ tsp chilli powder
4 tsp tomato purée
8 fl oz (240ml) water
Small amount green dhanyia (coriander), chopped

Method   *Preparation and cooking time: 35 mins.*

1. Wash the potatoes well.

2. Boil the potatoes, peel them and cut into ½ inch (2.5cm) cubes.

3. Melt the butter in a large pan and add the onion and chillies. Stir and cook the onion and chillies until the onion is light brown. Now add the turmeric powder, ginger powder, dhanyia powder, salt, chilli powder, and tomato purée. Stir continuously and cook for about 2 minutes. Add half of the water, stir, and add the potatoes. Mix well and let it cook for about 3 minutes.

4. Add the remaining water and bring it to the boil. Lower the heat and simmer gently for about 5 minutes.

5. Place the curry in a serving dish and garnish with fresh dhanyia.

GUJARATI GREEN BEAN CURRY

A large proportion of the residents of the Gujarat state of India are vegetarians and they have therefore improvised on many of the standard dhal and vegetable dishes. Green beans are one of their specialities.

Ingredients *Serves 4*

2 fl oz (60ml) cooking oil
½ tsp whole rai (black mustard seeds)
½ tsp whole jeera (cumin seeds)
¼ tsp hing (asafoetida)
2 oz (55g) fresh tomatoes, finely chopped
½ tsp salt
½ tsp turmeric powder
½ tsp jeera powder (cumin)
½ tsp dhanyia powder (coriander)
½ tsp chilli powder
12 oz (340g) frozen green beans (thawed)
4 fl oz (120ml) water

Method *Preparation and cooking time: 15 mins.*

1. Heat the oil to a high temperature, in a large pan. Add rai, jeera and asafoetida and let it cook for a few seconds. Add tomatoes, salt, turmeric powder, jeera powder, dhanyia powder and chilli powder. Let this spice mixture cook for about 2 minutes.

2. Add the beans, mix well and then add the water. Bring the water to the boil, lower the heat and let the beans simmer for about 8 minutes stirring every 2 to 3 minutes.

3. Transfer the contents to a serving dish and serve hot.

CAULIFLOWER AND POTATO CURRY (Dry)

This is a mild vegetable curry, especially good when served with a meat and dhal dish. It is also very popular with vegetarians. It is usually served with rice, chapattis or bread.

Ingredients   *Serves 4*

12 oz (340g) potatoes
12 oz (340g) cauliflower (1 medium cauliflower)
2 fl oz (60ml) cooking oil
½ tsp whole jeera (cumin seeds)
½ tsp whole rai (black mustard seeds)
1 tsp turmeric powder
1 tsp garam masala
2 tsp tomato purée
1 tsp salt
½ tsp chilli powder
4 fl oz (120ml) water
Small amount green dhanyia (coriander), chopped

Method   *Preparation and cooking time: 35 mins.*

1. Peel the potatoes and cut them into 1 inch (2.5cm) cubes.

2. Cut the cauliflower into small florets.

3. Heat the oil to a high temperature, in a pan. Add jeera and rai and leave to cook for a few seconds. Add potatoes, cauliflower, turmeric powder, garam masala, tomato purée, salt and chilli powder. Stir continuously and cook for about 3 minutes.

4. Add the water, bring it to the boil and simmer gently for about 15 minutes.

5. Place the curry in a serving dish and garnish with fresh dhanyia.

FRESH MIXED VEGETABLE CURRY

This is a very hot vegetable curry usually served with rice. For this recipe you need a liquidiser.

Ingredients   *Serves 4*

12 oz (340g) potatoes
1 large aubergine approx 8 oz (225g)
4 oz (110g) plum peeled tomatoes
1 oz (25g) fresh garlic (peeled)
2 oz (55g) fresh ginger (peeled)
2 fl oz (60ml) cooking oil
½ tsp whole jeera (cumin seeds)
½ tsp whole rai (black mustard seeds)
½ tsp turmeric powder
1 tsp garam masala
1½ tsp salt
¾ tsp chilli powder
8 green chillies
6 oz (170g) frozen peas (thawed)
20 fl oz (600ml) water
Small portion of fresh green dhanyia (coriander)

Method   *Preparation and cooking time: 45 mins.*

1. Peel the potatoes and cut them into 1 inch (2.5cm) cubes.

2. Remove the stalk of the aubergine and cut into 1 inch (2.5cm) cubes.

3. Place the tomatoes, garlic, and ginger into a liquidiser and blend into a thickish paste.

4. Heat the oil to a high temperature, in a pan. Add jeera and rai and leave it cooking for a few seconds. Add the thick paste, turmeric powder, garam masala, salt, chilli powder, potatoes, aubergine, green chillies and peas. Stir continuously and cook for about 5 minutes.

5. Add the water, bring it to the boil and simmer gently for about 30 minutes.

6. Place the curry in a serving dish and garnish with fresh dhanyia.

AUBERGINE AND POTATO CURRY (Dry)

This is a mild vegetable curry, especially good when served with a meat dish. It is also excellent for vegetarians. It is usually served with rice or chapattis. Parsley or fresh coriander can be used for garnishing.

Ingredients   *Serves 4*

1 lb (450g) potatoes
1 large aubergine approx 8 oz (225g)
2 large onions
2 fl oz (60ml) cooking oil
½ tsp whole jeera (cumin seeds)
½ tsp whole rai (black mustard seeds)
2 tsp tomato purée
1 tsp salt
½ tsp turmeric powder
½ tsp chilli powder
1 tsp tandoori masala
1 tsp garam masala
3 fl oz (90ml) water
Fresh parsley or green fresh dhanyia (coriander), finely
  chopped

Method   *Preparation and cooking time: 35 mins.*

1. Peel the potatoes and cut them into large chips.

2. Remove the stalk and cut the aubergine into large chip type pieces also.

3. Chop the onions into small pieces.

4. Heat the oil to a high temperature, in a large pan. Add the jeera and rai to the oil and cook until they are golden brown. This will only take a few seconds.

5. Add the chopped onions. Cook together until the onions are golden brown. Add the tomato purée, salt, turmeric powder, chilli powder, tandoori masala, garam

masala, potatoes and aubergine pieces. Stir and cook for another few minutes. Reduce the heat.

6. Add the water; bring to the boil, cover the pan and simmer gently for about 30 to 35 minutes, stirring every 5 to 7 minutes. Switch off the heat and place the cooked curry in a serving dish.

7. Garnish with parsley or fresh coriander.

AUBERGINE AND PEA CURRY

This is a mild curry usually served with chapattis, parothas or another meat dish.

Ingredients   *Serves 4*

1 lb (450g) aubergines
20 fl oz (600ml) water for soaking
2 fl oz (60ml) cooking oil
½ tsp whole rai (black mustard seeds)
½ tsp whole jeera (cumin seeds)
2 tsp tomato purée
1 tsp turmeric powder
1 tsp salt
1 tsp chilli powder
1 tsp garam masala
1 tsp garlic powder
4 fl oz (120ml) water
8 oz (225g) frozen peas
2 tsp lemon juice
Small amount green dhanyia (coriander), chopped

Method   *Preparation and cooking time: 25 mins.*

1. Remove the stalks from the aubergines and slice them lengthways, like large chips. Soak the aubergines in the 20 fluid ounces of water for about 5 minutes.

2. Heat the oil to a high temperature, in a heavy-based saucepan. Add the whole rai and whole jeera and let it cook for a few seconds.

3. Remove the aubergines from the water and add them to the pot. Now add the tomato purée, turmeric powder, salt, chilli powder, garam masala and garlic powder. Mix well and cook for about 2 to 3 minutes.

4. Add the 4 fluid ounces of water, cover the pan, reduce the heat and let the aubergines simmer for about 10 minutes stirring every 4 to 5 minutes.

5. Add the peas and the lemon juice. Simmer for a further 7 minutes stirring every 3 to 4 minutes.

6. Transfer the contents to a serving dish and serve while hot.

AUBERGINE AND SPINACH BHARTHA
(M ashed aubergine and spinach)

Bharthas are usually served with chapattis or as a side dish. This is a hot vegetable dish.

Ingredients   *Serves 4*

1 lb (450g) aubergines
1 lb (450g) fresh spinach
2 fl oz (60ml) cooking oil
1 large onion, finely chopped
4 oz (110g) plum peeled tomatoes, finely chopped
1 tsp salt
1 tsp turmeric powder
1 tsp chilli powder
1 tsp dhanyia powder (coriander)
1 tsp jeera powder (cumin)
1 tsp garlic powder

Method　　*Preparation and cooking time: 1 hr. 10 mins.*

1. Prick the aubergines with a fork and then roast them under the grill for about 30 minutes, turning every 7 to 8 minutes. When the aubergines have been well roasted, remove the stalks, peel the aubergines and cut into very small pieces or mash them.

2. Wash the spinach, and chop finely.

3. Heat the oil to a high temperature, in a large pan. Add the onion and cook, stirring continuously, until the onion is golden brown. Add the mashed aubergine, spinach, tomatoes, salt, turmeric powder, chilli powder, dhanyia powder, jeera powder, and garlic powder. Stir and mix well. Lower the heat, cover the pan and let it simmer for about 25 minutes stirring every 5 to 7 minutes.

4. Transfer the contents to a serving dish and serve while hot.

FRESH SPINACH CURRY

If you like spinach, then you must try this dish. It can be served instead of boiled spinach or, like other vegetable curries, with chapattis or a side dish.

Ingredients　　　　　　　　　　　　　　　　*Serves 4*

2 fl oz (60ml) cooking oil
1 small onion, finely chopped
1 lb (450g) fresh spinach, finely chopped
½ tsp turmeric powder
½ tsp chilli powder
½ tsp salt
½ tsp garam masala
½ tsp garlic powder
1 tsp tomato purée
1 tomato, cut into small pieces

Method ·   *Preparation and cooking time: 25 mins.*

1. Heat the oil to a high temperature, in a large pan. Add the onion and cook until the onion is golden brown. Add the spinach, turmeric powder, chilli powder, salt, garam masala, garlic powder and tomato purée. Mix well, cover the pan, lower the heat, and let it simmer for about 15 minutes, stirring every 4 to 5 minutes.

2. Transfer the spinach to a serving dish and garnish with the tomato.

GREEN PEPPER WITH NEW POTATO CURRY

This is a very mild vegetable curry and can be served with chapattis, or dhal curries and rice. It tastes especially good with new potatoes, but ordinary potatoes can be used.

Ingredients   *Serves 4*

2 fl oz (60ml) cooking oil
½ tsp whole jeera (cumin seeds)
1 onion, finely chopped
8 oz (225g) new potatoes, peeled and cut into very thin
   discs, like crisps
2 large green peppers, sliced in rings like crisps
1 tsp salt
½ tsp turmeric powder
½ tsp garam masala
3 fl oz (90ml) water
1 tsp tomato purée
½ tsp chilli powder

Method   *Preparation and cooking time: 35 mins.*

1. Heat the oil to a high temperature in a wok or a deep

pan. Add the jeera, cook for a few seconds and add the onion. Cook until golden brown.

2. Add the potatoes, peppers, salt, turmeric powder, garam masala, water, tomato purée, and the chilli powder. Mix well.

3. Bring the water to the boil, lower the heat and cover the pan. Simmer gently for about 20 minutes, stirring every 5 to 7 minutes.

4. Transfer the contents to serving dish and serve while hot.

WHITE CABBAGE CURRY

This is a hot vegetable curry usually served with a rice dish, or chapattis. It also makes an excellent filling for toasted sandwiches. For this recipe you need a liquidiser.

Ingredients   *Serves 4*

1 oz (25g) fresh garlic (peeled)
2 oz (55g) fresh ginger (peeled)
6 whole green chillies
2 fl oz (60ml) cooking oil
½ tsp whole jeera (cumin seeds)
½ tsp whole rai (black mustard seeds)
4 whole cloves
4 whole black peppercorns
¼ tsp hing (asafoetida)
1½ lb (670g) white cabbage, shredded
2 tsp tomato purée
½ tsp turmeric powder
½ tsp chilli powder
1 tsp garam masala
1 tsp salt
4 tsp soy sauce
6 fl oz (180ml) water

Method   *Preparation and cooking time: 40 mins.*

1. Place the garlic, ginger, and green chillies in a liquidiser, and chop finely.

2. Heat the oil to a high temperature in a wok or large pan, and add jeera, rai, whole cloves, whole peppercorns, and asafoetida. Cook for a few seconds.

3. Add the cabbage, tomato purée, turmeric powder, chilli powder, garam masala, salt and soy sauce. Cook for a further few seconds.

4. Add the contents of the liquidiser and water to the cabbage.

5. Stir well and bring the mixture to the boil. Cover the pan, reduce the heat and simmer gently for about 20 minutes, stirring every 5 to 7 minutes.

6. Transfer the contents to a serving dish and serve hot.

7. The cloves are discarded and left at the side of the plate while eating.

TINDORA CURRY

This is a very unusual curry, and tastes like courgettes or cucumber. If you are prepared to try something new, then this may be to your taste. It is usually served with rice or chapattis. For this recipe you need a liquidiser.

Ingredients   *Serves 4*

3 oz (85g) fresh garlic (peeled)
3 oz (85g) fresh ginger (peeled)
4 whole green chillies
1 lb (450g) fresh tindora (see introduction, page 17)
2 fl oz (60ml) cooking oil
½ tsp whole jeera (cumin seeds)

(continued overleaf)

(contd from p. 119)
½ tsp whole rai (black mustard seeds)
¼ tsp hing (asafoetida)
2 tsp tomato purée
1 tsp salt
½ tsp turmeric powder
1 tsp chilli powder
1 tsp garam masala
4 tsp soy sauce
10 fl oz (300ml) water
1 fresh tomato, cut into small pieces for garnishing

Method   *Preparation and cooking time: 20 mins.*

1. Place the garlic, ginger, and green chillies into a liquidiser and chop finely.

2. Cut each fresh tindora into four pieces.

3. Heat the oil to a high temperature, in a large pan, and add jeera, rai and asafoetida. Fry for a few seconds.

4. Add the cut tindora, contents of the liquidiser, tomato purée, salt, turmeric powder, chilli powder, garam masala and soy sauce. Stir and cook for about 2 minutes. Add the water, and bring to the boil. Reduce the heat, cover the pan and simmer gently for about 7 minutes.

5. Transfer the contents to a serving dish and garnish with the tomato.

VALLOUR VEGETABLE CURRY

This is an unusual vegetable curry and tastes very similar to courgettes. It is usually served with chapattis or with another dhal curry and rice.

Ingredients   *Serves 4*

2 medium size potatoes
12 oz (340g) fresh vallour (see introduction, page 17)

2 fl oz (60ml) cooking oil
1 tsp whole rai (black mustard seeds)
1 tsp whole jeera (cumin seeds)
¼ tsp hing (asafoetida)
2 tsp tomato purée
½ tsp chilli powder
1 tsp salt
1½ tsp garam masala
½ tsp turmeric powder
1 tsp garlic powder
1 tsp tandoori masala
10 fl oz (300ml) water
1 fresh tomato, cut into small pieces for garnishing

Method   *Preparation and cooking time: 35 mins.*

1. Peel the potatoes and cut into about 1 inch (2.5cm) cubes.

2. Top and tail the vallour and cut them lengthways into about 1 inch (2.5cm) long pieces.

3. Heat the oil in a wok or pan and add rai, jeera and asafoetida. Cook for a few seconds. Add the potatoes, vallour, tomato purée, chilli powder, salt, garam masala, turmeric powder, garlic powder and tandoori masala. Stir continuously and cook for a further 5 minutes.

4. Add the water; bring it to the boil, reduce the heat and simmer gently for a further 20 minutes.

5. Transfer the contents to a serving dish and garnish with the tomato. Serve while hot.

GUAER CURRY

It is difficult to describe the flavour of guaer. The closest approximation is that it tastes similar to green beans.

Ingredients   *Serves 4*

8 oz (225g) guaer (see introduction, page 17)
2 fl oz (60ml) cooking oil
½ tsp whole rai (black mustard seeds)
½ tsp whole jeera (cumin seeds)
¼ tsp hing (asafoetida)
2 tsp tomato purée
1 tsp salt
1 tsp turmeric powder
1 tsp jeera powder (cumin)
1 tsp dhanyia powder (coriander)
1 tsp chilli powder
15 fl oz (450ml) water

Method   *Preparation and cooking time: 45 mins.*

1. Top and tail the guaer and then cut into about 1 inch (2cm) lengths.

2. Heat the oil to a high temperature, in a large pan. Add rai, jeera and asafoetida and let it cook for a few seconds. Add tomato purée, salt, turmeric powder, jeera powder, dhanyia powder and chilli powder. Let this spice mixture cook for about 2 minutes.

3. Add the guaer, mix well and then add the water. Lower the heat and let the guaer simmer for about 30 minutes stirring every 5 to 6 minutes.

4. Transfer the contents to a serving dish and serve hot.

KADU AND TOMATO CURRY

Kadu tastes somewhat similar to marrow. This is a very mild curry usually served with chapattis.

Ingredients   *Serves 4*

8 oz (225g) kadu (see introduction, page 17)
2 fl oz (60ml) cooking oil
½ tsp whole rai (black mustard seeds)
½ tsp whole jeera (cumin seeds)
4 oz (110g) fresh tomatoes, finely chopped
½ tsp salt
½ tsp turmeric powder
½ tsp garam masala
½ tsp chilli powder

Method   *Preparation and cooking time: 25 mins.*

1. Peel the kadu and cut into about 1 inch (2cm) cubes.

2. Heat the oil to a high temperature, in a large pan. Add rai and jeera and let it cook for a few seconds. Add tomatoes, salt, turmeric powder, garam masala and chilli powder. Let this spice mixture cook for about 1 minute.

3. Add the kadu. Lower the heat and let the kadu simmer for about 30 minutes stirring every 5 to 7 minutes.

4. Transfer the contents to a serving dish. Serve hot.

6 RAITAS, CHUTNEYS AND PICKLES

PLAIN FRESH NATURAL YOGHURT

Raitas, made from fresh natural yoghurt, are very common in Indian homes. Most Indians make fresh yoghurt themselves, and fresh yoghurt made at home tastes different. Yoghurt is usually made in the evenings and left to 'set' overnight. Raita can then be made in the morning.

Ingredients   *Makes 20 fl oz (600 ml)*

20 fl oz (600ml) milk
1 fl oz (30ml) natural yoghurt

Method   *Preparation and cooking time: 8 hrs. 30 mins.*

1. Bring the milk to the boil in a large pan. Leave it to cool

for about 10 minutes, so that the milk is warm, before going to the next step.

2. Transfer the milk into a bowl with a cover. Add the yoghurt and mix well. Cover the bowl and leave the mixture in a warm place, such as the airing cupboard, for about 8 hours.

3. The setting process may take longer than 8 hours if the temperature is not warm enough.

POTATO AND ONION RAITA

All raitas are served as side dishes and are especially good in the summer.

Ingredients   *Serves 4*

12 oz (340g) boiled potatoes
1 large onion, finely chopped
1 green chilli, finely chopped
15 fl oz (450ml) plain, fresh natural yoghurt
3 fl oz (90ml) cold, fresh milk
½ tsp salt
½ tsp chilli powder
½ tsp black pepper

Method   *Preparation and cooking time: 30 mins.*

1. Cut the boiled potatoes into small pieces.

2. Place the potatoes, onion and green chilli into a serving dish. Add the yoghurt and milk, and mix well.

3. Place the raita in a fridge.

4. When you are ready to serve, remove the raita from the fridge and add the salt, chilli powder and black pepper. Mix well and serve.

ONION AND CUCUMBER RAITA

Ingredients   *Serves 4*

15 fl oz (450ml) plain fresh natural yoghurt
3 fl oz (90ml) cold milk
4 oz (110g) cucumber, peeled and sliced
1 large onion, chopped into small pieces
½ tsp whole jeera (cumin seeds)
½ tsp salt
½ tsp chilli powder
½ tsp black ground pepper

Method   *Preparation and cooking time: 15 mins.*

1. Combine the yoghurt and milk in a serving dish and mix well.

2. Add the sliced cucumber, onion and whole jeera. Mix well.

3. Place the raita in a fridge.

4. When ready to serve, mix salt, chilli powder and black ground pepper into the raita.

GARLIC CHUTNEY

Garlic chutneys are not served at meals but are used in cooking many curry dishes. Instead of blending garlic and ginger in a liquidiser, a spoonful of garlic chutney can be used instead. This saves having to peel garlic and ginger every time. You need a liquidiser to prepare this chutney.

Ingredients   *Makes about 1 lb (450g) of chutney*

2 fl oz (60ml) water
4 oz (110g) green chillies

6 oz (170g) fresh ginger (peeled)
4 oz (110g) fresh garlic (peeled)
1½ tsp salt
2 fl oz (60ml) lemon juice

Method   *Preparation and cooking time: 40 mins.*

1. Place all the ingredients in a liquidiser and blend together.

2. Transfer the contents into a jar, and store in a fridge. This chutney can be kept for up to 3 weeks.

FRESH MINT CHUTNEY

This is a mild chutney, often served with main meals. Sugar can be added to give it a slightly sweeter taste. Either anardana or lemon can be used. A liquidiser or blender is needed to prepare this chutney.

Ingredients   *Serves 4*

2 oz (55g) fresh mint leaves
1 small onion, finely chopped
½ tsp salt
½ tsp whole jeera (cumin seeds)
½ tsp sugar (optional)
½ tsp anardana (pomegranate seeds) or ½ tsp lemon juice
½ oz (10g) green chillies
1 fl oz (30ml) water

Method   *Preparation and cooking time: 15 mins.*

1. Place all the ingredients in a liquidiser and blend them into a smooth paste.

2. Transfer the contents to a serving dish.

3. Like all chutneys this can be stored in a cool place and served again. This chutney must be used in 3 to 4 days.

FRESH MINT AND APPLE CHUTNEY

Chutneys are usually served with all main meals as a small side dish, like pickles. This is a hot chutney and is very good with most rice dishes. Sugar can be added to give it a slightly sweeter taste. A liquidiser or blender is needed to prepare this chutney.

Ingredients   *Serves 4*

2 oz (55g) mint leaves
4 oz (110g) cooking apples, finely chopped
2 oz (55g) onions, finely chopped
2 oz (55g) green chillies
¾ tsp salt
1 fl oz (30ml) water
½ tsp turmeric powder
½ tsp sugar (optional)

Method   *Preparation and cooking time: 15 mins.*

1. Place all the ingredients in a liquidiser and blend them into a smooth paste.

2. Transfer the contents into a small serving dish and place in the fridge for a couple of hours.

3. The chutney is ready to be served. Unused chutney can be left in the fridge, and served again. This chutney must be used within 7 days.

GREEN CHILLI PICKLE (Fried)

Sugar can be added to give the pickle a slightly sweeter taste.

Ingredients   *Serves 4*

2 oz (55g) green chillies
1 fl oz (30ml) cooking oil
¼ tsp whole jeera (cumin seeds)
¼ tsp whole rai (black mustard seeds)
¼ tsp hing (asafoetida)
½ tsp salt
½ tsp turmeric powder
½ fl oz (15ml) lemon juice
½ tsp sugar (optional)
2 fl oz (30ml) water

Method   *Preparation and cooking time: 20 mins.*

1. Remove the stems and slice the chillies into halves lengthways. (Remember to wash hands thoroughly after handling the chillies otherwise the chillies leave a burning sensation on hands.)

2. Place the cooking oil in a frying pan. Heat the oil to a high temperature; add jeera, rai, and asafoetida. Leave to cook for a few seconds until they are slightly brown. Add the chillies, salt, turmeric powder, lemon juice, sugar (if used) and water. Bring to the boil. Reduce the heat and simmer for about 5 minutes.

3. Place the cooked chillies in a serving dish.

FRESH GREEN CHILLI PICKLE

Ingredients   *Serves 4*

2 oz (55g) green chillies
1½ tsp salt
1½ tsp rai dhal (split black mustard)
½ tsp turmeric powder

(continued overleaf)

(contd from p. 129)
1 tsp cooking oil
2 fl oz (60ml) lemon juice
¼ tsp hing (asafoetida)

Method   *Preparation and cooking time: 10 mins.*

1. Remove the stems and slice the chillies into halves lengthways. (Remember to wash hands thoroughly after handling the chillies otherwise they leave a burning sensation on the hands.)

2. Mix well all the ingredients together with the cut chillies in a large bowl, and then transfer the contents to an airtight tin.

3. This pickle can be stored for up to 2 weeks if kept in an airtight tin and placed in the fridge. Use as and when needed.

LEMON AND GREEN CHILLI PICKLE

This is a pickle in which lemon and fresh green chillies are allowed to marinate in their own juices for about 3–4 days. It is not spicy, but very hot.

Ingredients   *Serves 4*

2 oz (55g) green chillies
4 tsp salt for green chillies
2 fresh lemons
1 tsp salt for lemons

Method   *Preparation and cooking time: 4 days*

1. Remove the stems and cut open one side of the chillies along the length, so that the chillies still remain whole. (Remember to wash hands thoroughly after handling the

chillies otherwise they leave a burning sensation on hands.)

2. With a teaspoon fill the chillies with salt. The four teaspoonsfuls of salt should be enough to fill all the chillies.

3. Slice the lemons into quarters, but do not cut them right through. Leave about a quarter of an inch (½cm) at the bottom where the lemon is not cut. Ensure that the lemon still remains in one piece.

4. Now share the teaspoonful of salt between the two lemons.

5. Transfer both the lemons and the chillies to an airtight tin and leave it in a cool place (not the fridge) for about 4 days. The salt will draw out the juices from the lemons and chillies and these will marinate in their own juices.

6. This pickle can be stored for up to 2 weeks if kept in an airtight tin and placed in the fridge. Use as and when needed.

CARROT, WHITE CABBAGE AND GREEN CHILLI PICKLE

Of the many Indian pickles served with main meals, this is one of the few prepared fresh, and served hot. Sugar can be added to give the pickle a slightly sweeter taste.

Ingredients   *Serves 4*

1 fl oz (30ml) cooking oil
¼ tsp whole jeera (cumin seeds)
¼ tsp whole rai (black mustard seeds)
¼ tsp hing (asafoetida)
4 small green chillies cut into halves lengthways
2 oz (55g) white cabbage, shredded
4 small carrots, cut into long, thin strips

(continued overleaf)

(contd from p. 131)
1 tsp sugar (optional)
½ tsp salt
½ tsp turmeric powder
½ tsp tomato purée
3 fl oz (90ml) water
1 fl oz (30ml) lemon juice

Method   *Preparation and cooking time: 30 mins.*

1. Heat the oil to a high temperature, in a frying pan, and add the jeera, rai and asafoetida. Cook for a few seconds.

2. Add the chillies, cabbage, carrots, sugar (if used), salt, turmeric powder and tomato purée and cook for a further 2 minutes, stirring continuously. Add the water, and bring the mixture to the boil. Reduce the heat, and simmer gently until the water has evaporated. This will take about 15 minutes. Add the lemon juice and cook for a further 1 minute stirring all the time.

3. Transfer the contents to a serving dish.

CARROT PICKLE

Ingredients   *Serves 4*
8 oz (225g) carrots
1 tsp salt
½ tsp turmeric powder
1 fl oz (30ml) cooking oil
1 fl oz (30ml) lemon juice
2 tsp rai dhal (split mustard)
¼ tsp hing (asafoetida)

Method   *Preparation and cooking time: 15 mins.*

1. Peel the carrots; wash them and cut them into 1 inch

(2.5cm) long strips about quarter of an inch (½cm) thick.

2. Add all the above spices to the carrots, mix well, and transfer the contents to an airtight tin.

3. This pickle can be stored for up to 2 weeks if kept in an airtight tin and placed in the fridge. Use as and when needed.

APPLE PICKLE

Ingredients   *Serves 4*

8 oz (225g) cooking apples
½ fl oz (15ml) cooking oil
1 tsp salt
¼ tsp garam masala
¼ tsp ground jeera (cumin seeds)
½ tsp rai dhal (split mustard)
¼ tsp hing (asafoetida)
½ fl oz (15ml) lemon juice

Method   *Preparation and cooking time: 15 mins.*

1. Peel the apples and cut them into about ½ inch (1cm) cubes.

2. Heat the oil in a pan. Add the salt, garam masala, ground jeera, rai dhal and asafoetida. Cook for a few seconds.

3. Switch off the heat, add the apples and lemon juice and mix well.

4. Transfer the contents to an airtight tin.

5. This pickle can be stored for up to 1 week if kept in an airtight tin and placed in the fridge. Use as and when needed.

7 MISCELLANEOUS

CHAPATTIS

Chapattis are a good substitute for bread and can be served with almost any curry. For this recipe you need a large flat frying pan or tava.

Ingredients   *Makes about 15 chapattis*

1 lb (450g) white chapatti flour (sieved)
1 fl oz (30ml) cooking oil
7 fl oz (210ml) water
2 oz (55g) chapatti flour, for rolling
2 oz (55g) butter

Method   *Preparation and cooking time: 30 mins.*

1. Place the sieved flour in a bowl and add the cooking oil. Mix together for a few seconds.

2. Add water gradually, and continue to mix until a stiff or medium soft dough is formed, which can be kneaded.

3. Divide the mixture into about 15 balls, sprinkle flour on the rolling area and roll each ball into a disc of about seven inches diameter.

4. Heat a tava or large flat pan to a high temperature. Place the chapatti on it, leave it for a few seconds and turn it over. After a few seconds turn and cook the first side again, until it turns light brown in colour. Repeat for the other side. The cooking process takes approximately 15 seconds for each side. Remove the chapatti from the pan and place it on a plate. Butter one side of each chapatti, and stack one on top of another. Serve them hot.

BHATURAS

Bhaturas can be served with almost any curry dish, but are usually served with chana, and raita. They taste like very soft bread, and are served instead of chapattis or puris (deep fried chapattis). For this recipe you need a deep frying pan or wok.

Ingredients   *Serves 4*

1 lb (450g) plain flour, (sieved) for dough
1 tsp baking powder (sieved)
10 fl oz (300ml) plain yoghurt
2 oz (55g) plain flour, for rolling
20 fl oz (600ml) cooking oil, for deep frying

Method   *Preparation and cooking time: 4 hrs. 40 mins.*

1. Mix the flour, baking powder and yoghurt in a large mixing bowl, and make a medium soft dough. Leave the dough covered for 4 hours.

2. Divide the dough into about 12 equal parts.

3. Shape each part into a ball, flour the surface of the balls well with dry flour. Roll the balls flat into about quarter of an inch (½cm) thick, five to six inches (14cm) diameter discs.

4. Heat the oil to a high temperature in a wok or deep frying pan, and then reduce the heat. Deep fry the rolled bhatura, which will float, one at a time, for about ½ minute on each side. Drain the oil from the bhatura and place in a serving dish. Repeat this with all the bhaturas.

5. Serve hot.

PEA PILAW RICE

This is one of the many rice dishes usually served with any curry or dhal.

Ingredients   *Serves 4*

6 oz (170g) basmati rice
13 fl oz (390ml) water
2 fl oz (60ml) cooking oil
½ tsp whole jeera (cumin seeds)
½ tsp whole rai (black mustard seeds)
½ tsp salt
½ tsp turmeric powder
½ tsp chilli powder
1 tsp tomato purée
3 oz (85g) frozen peas

Method   *Preparation and cooking time: 1 hr. 30 mins.*

1. Wash the rice like a dhal as described in the introduction (page 16).

2. Soak the rice for about 1 hour in the 13 fluid ounces of water.

3. Heat the oil in a pan and add jeera and rai. Leave to cook for a few seconds.

4. Very carefully add the soaked rice and water, salt, turmeric powder, chilli powder, tomato purée, and peas. If they are added too quickly, the mixture will spit all over the place. Bring the mixture to the boil.

5. Reduce the heat, cover the pan and let it simmer gently for about 20 minutes.

6. Transfer the contents to a serving dish, and serve while hot.

FRIED RICE

Fried rice can feature as a snack or at high tea, without curry or dhals. Left over plain boiled rice can also be fried in the manner described below. For this recipe you need a large wok or deep frying pan.

Ingredients   *Serves 4*

6 oz (170g) plain basmati rice
50 fl oz (1500ml) water
2 fl oz (60ml) cooking oil
½ tsp whole rai (black mustard seeds)
½ tsp whole jeera (cumin seeds)
¼ tsp hing (asafoetida)
1 small onion, finely chopped
1 small potato, chopped into very small pieces
½ tsp turmeric powder
1 tsp salt
½ tsp chilli powder
1 large tomato, cut into round rings, for garnishing

Method   *Preparation and cooking time: 1 hr. 30 mins.*

1. Wash the rice and leave to soak in the 50 fluid ounces of

water for about 1 hour.

2. Bring the water containing the rice to the boil, and then simmer gently for a further 15 minutes.

3. Transfer the contents to a colander to drain the rice.

4. Heat the oil in a big wok or a deep frying pan. Add rai, jeera and asafoetida, and cook them for a few seconds. Add the onion and cook until it is golden brown. Add the potato and cook over a low heat for about 10 minutes. Make sure that the potato is well cooked.

5. Add the rice, turmeric powder, salt and chilli powder and stir well. Cook the whole mixture together for a further 3 minutes stirring continuously.

6. Transfer the contents to a serving dish. Garnish with the fresh tomato and serve hot.

CHICKEN BIRYANI

This is a mild rice dish, quick to make and popular with busy housewives. It is usually served with fresh salad. For this recipe you need a wok, or deep frying pan, and a liquidiser.

Ingredients   *Serves 4*

1 oz (25g) fresh garlic (peeled)
2 oz (55g) fresh ginger (peeled)
30 fl oz (900ml) chicken stock
6 oz (170g) basmati rice
3 large chicken pieces
4 fl oz (120ml) cooking oil
3 whole cloves
4 whole black peppercorns
½ tsp whole jeera (cumin seeds)
½ tsp whole rai (black mustard seeds)

¼ tsp hing (asafoetida)
1 onion, finely chopped
1 tsp tomato purée
3 oz (85g) frozen peas
1 small carrot, sliced thinly
½ tsp turmeric powder
1 tsp salt
½ tsp chilli powder

Method *Preparation and cooking time: 1 hr. 20 mins.*

1. Place the garlic and ginger in a liquidiser and chop finely. Add the contents of the liquidiser to the 30 fluid ounces of chicken stock and mix well.

2. Wash the rice like all dhals (see page 16).

3. Remove the skin and bones from the chicken and cut the chicken into small pieces, about 3 inches long.

4. Heat 2 fluid ounces of cooking oil to a high temperature in a wok or deep frying pan; add the chicken pieces and cook over a low heat until the chicken pieces are golden brown.

5. In another separate pan heat the remaining 2 fluid ounces of oil to a high temperature. Add cloves, pepper-corns, jeera, rai, and asafoetida and cook for a few seconds. Add the chopped onion, and cook until the onion is golden brown. Add rice, cooked chicken, tomato purée, peas, carrot, turmeric powder, salt and chilli powder. Cook for a further 2 minutes, stirring con-tinuously.

6. Add the stock mixture to the rice. Bring it to the boil and reduce the heat. Cover the pan and simmer gently for about 15 minutes. The rice should now look pretty dry.

7. Transfer the contents to a serving dish and serve while hot.

8. The cloves and peppercorns are discarded while eating and left on the plate.

LAMB BIRYANI

This is a mild rice dish, usually served with dhal or a vegetable dish.

Ingredients   *Serves 4*

6 oz (170g) basmati rice
25 fl oz (750ml) water
1 small onion, finely chopped
1 green chilli, finely chopped
8 oz (225g) boneless lamb, cut into very small ½ in (1cm) cubes
½ tsp turmeric powder
1 tsp salt
½ tsp chilli powder
2 tsp soy sauce
3 oz (85g) frozen peas
3 oz (85g) frozen diced carrots

Method   *Preparation and cooking time: 1 hr.*

1. Wash the rice like all dhals, as described in the introduction.

2. In a large pan mix the water, onion, green chilli, lamb, turmeric powder, salt, chilli powder, and soy sauce. Bring to the boil, cover the pan, reduce the heat and let the mixture boil for about 35 minutes.

3. Add the washed rice, peas and carrots. Bring back to the boil and then reduce the heat again. Cover the pan and simmer gently for about 12 minutes. The rice, should look dry.

4. Transfer the contents to a serving dish and serve hot.

VEGETABLE BIRYANI

If you like rice and are a vegetarian, then vegetable biryani is just the thing for you. It is usually served with fresh salad. For this recipe you need a deep frying pan, or wok, and a liquidiser.

Ingredients   *Serves 4*

6 oz (170g) basmati rice
1 oz (25g) fresh garlic (peeled)
1 oz (25g) fresh ginger (peeled)
2 fl oz (60ml) cooking oil
3 whole cloves
½ tsp whole jeera (cumin seeds)
½ tsp whole rai (black mustard seeds)
¼ tsp hing (asafoetida)
1 large onion, finely chopped
1 tsp tomato purée
4 oz (110g) frozen peas
6 oz (170g) frozen diced carrots (properly thawed)
8 oz (225g) frozen cauliflower (properly thawed)
1 large potato, finely chopped
½ tsp turmeric powder
1 tsp salt
½ tsp chilli powder
20 fl oz (600ml) water

Method   *Preparation and cooking time: 40 mins.*

1. Wash the rice, like dhals as described in the introduction.

2. Place the garlic and ginger in a liquidiser, and chop finely.

3. Heat the oil to a high temperature, in a wok or deep frying pan. Add cloves, jeera, rai and asafoetida, and cook for a few seconds. Add the chopped onion, and cook

until the onion is golden brown.

4. Add the contents of the liquidiser and cook for a further 2 minutes. Add the tomato purée, peas, carrots, cauliflower, potato, turmeric powder, salt and chilli powder. Cook for a further 2 minutes, stirring continuously.

5. Add the water and rice. Bring the mixture to the boil and reduce the heat. Cover the pan and simmer gently for about 15 minutes. The rice should now look dry.

6. Transfer the contents to a serving dish and serve while hot.

PURIS

Puris are very similar to chapattis but are deep fried. This deep frying process gives them a slightly different taste from chapattis. For this recipe you need a deep frying pan or wok.

Ingredients   *Makes about 25 puris*

1 lb (450g) white chapatti flour (sieved)
1 fl oz (30ml) cooking oil
7 fl oz (210ml) water
2 oz (55g) chapatti flour, for rolling
40 fl oz (1200ml) cooking oil, for deep frying

Method   *Preparation and cooking time: 50 mins.*

1. Place the sieved flour in the bowl and add the 1 fluid ounce cooking oil. Mix together for a few seconds.

2. Add the water gradually, and continue to mix, until a medium soft dough is formed which can be kneaded.

3. Divide the mixture into about 25 balls. Sprinkle flour on the rolling area and roll each ball flat into a round shape about 5 inches (12cm) in diameter.

4. Heat the oil to a high temperature, in a deep frying pan

or wok. Once the oil is hot keep it at a steady temperature, at about medium heat. Place the rolled puri in the oil and fry for about 20 seconds. Now turn and fry the other side for about the same time. The puri should turn golden brown. If the colour changes to golden brown very quickly, then lower the heat.

5. You may find it easier to roll out all the puris first, lay them out separately, and then deep fry them individually. Once you get used to the process then both rolling and frying can be done concurrently.

6. Serve the puris hot.

PLAIN PAROTHAS

Parothas can be served with most curries. They are heavy in calories. They taste nice cold and are therefore useful for picnics etc. For this recipe you need a large flat frying pan or tava.

Ingredients   *Makes about 16 parothas*

2 lb (900g) white chapatti flour (sieved)
2 fl oz (60ml) cooking oil
14 fl oz (420ml) water
4 oz (110g) chapatti flour, for rolling
16 fl oz (480ml) cooking oil, for frying parothas

Method   *Preparation and cooking time: 40 mins.*

1. Mix the sieved flour and the 2 fluid ounces of cooking oil in a bowl and leave it for a few seconds.

2. Add the water gradually to the above mixture, and continue to mix well, until a medium stiff dough is formed.

3. Divide the above mixture into about 16 roughly equal

portions. Sprinkle flour onto a rolling area and roll the balls into discs about five inches (12cm) in diameter.

4. Spread a teaspoonful of cooking oil onto the flat rolled chapatti, and sprinkle a little bit of dry flour on top. Fold the chapatti first into halves and then into quarters. Roll out each shape as a triangle, with one curved side, such that the straight sides are about five inches (12cm) long.

5. Heat a tava or flat pan and place the rolled parotha on the pan. Leave it for a few seconds. Now turn it over and cook the other side for a few seconds. Turn it back again and cook for a further few seconds.

6. Now spread a teaspoonful of cooking oil on the top of the cooking parotha and turn it over so that the oiled side is underneath. Spread the other side similarly with cooking oil and turn again to cook the second side. Continue cooking until both sides of the parotha are light brown. Remove the parotha from the pan and place it in a dish.

7. Cook all the parothas in this way.

PAROTHAS STUFFED WITH POTATOES

Unlike plain parothas, stuffed parothas are often eaten without curries and are cooked for high teas or picnics. Potato stuffed parothas are a favourite with children. For this recipe you need a large flat frying pan or tava.

Ingredients   *Makes about 16 parothas*

2 lb (900g) potatoes (skin peeled)
1 tsp salt
½ tsp garam masala
½ tsp chilli powder
¼ tsp jeera (cumin seeds)
Small amount green dhanyia, (coriander), chopped

2 lb (900g) white, chapatti flour (sieved)
2 fl oz (60ml) cooking oil
14 fl oz (420ml) water
4 oz (110g) chapatti flour, for rolling
16 fl oz (480ml) cooling oil, for frying parothas

Method   *Preparation and cooking time: 1 hr.*

1. Boil the potatoes, as if you were making mash.

2. Mash the potatoes and add salt, garam masala, chilli powder, jeera and the fresh green coriander. Mix everything well.

3. Mix the sieved flour and the 2 fluid ounces of cooking oil in a bowl and leave it for a few seconds.

4. Add the water gradually, to the above mixture and continue to mix well, until a medium stiff dough is formed.

5. Divide the dough into about 16 roughly equal portions and shape them into balls. Sprinkle flour onto a rolling area and roll the balls into discs about five inches (12cm) in diameter.

6. Place two large tablespoonfuls of the spiced mash onto the flat rolled chapatti, and sprinkle a little bit of dry flour on top. Fold the chapatti into a ball so that the mash is completely covered by the dough. Roll out the balls again into discs, about seven inches (17cm) in diameter.

7. Heat a tava or flat pan to a high temperature and place the rolled parotha on the pan. Leave it for a few seconds. Now turn it over and cook the other side for a few seconds. Turn it back again and cook for a further few seconds.

8. Now spread a teaspoonful of cooking oil on the top of the cooking parotha and turn it over so that the oiled side is underneath. Spread the other side similarly with the

cooking oil and turn again to cook the second side. Continue cooking until both sides of the parotha are light brown. Remove the parotha from the pan and place it in a dish.

9. Cook all the parothas in this way.

PAROTHAS STUFFED WITH CAULIFLOWER

Stuffed parothas do not need curries and they are often cooked for high teas or picnics. Cauliflower stuffed parothas are very different and sometimes served for breakfast, in the northern parts of India. For this recipe you need a large flat frying pan or tava and a grater.

Ingredients   *Makes about 8 parothas*

1 lb (450g) cauliflower
½ tsp salt
½ tsp garam masala
½ tsp chilli powder
1 lb (450g) white chapatti flour (sieved)
1 fl oz (30ml) cooking oil
7 fl oz (210ml) water
4 oz (110g) chapatti flour, for rolling
8 fl oz (240ml) cooking oil, for frying parothas

Method   *Preparation and cooking time: 1 hr.*

1. Cut and wash the cauliflower and then grate it.

2. Mix the cauliflower, salt, garam masala and the chilli powder. After mixing, squeeze out all the water from the grated spiced cauliflower.

3. Mix the sieved flour and the 1 fluid ounce of cooking oil

in a bowl and leave it for a few seconds.

4. Add water gradually, to the above mixture and continue to mix well, until a medium stiff dough is formed. Leave the dough in a cool place for about 30 minutes.

5. Divide the dough into about 8 roughly equal portions and shape them into balls. Sprinkle flour onto a rolling area and roll the balls into discs about six inches (15cm) in diameter.

6. Place two tablespoonfuls of spiced cauliflower onto the flat rolled chapatti, and sprinkle a little bit of dry flour on top. Fold the chapatti into a ball in such a way that the cauliflower is completely covered by the dough. Roll out the balls again into discs, about seven inches (17cm) in diameter.

7. Heat a tava or flat pan to a high temperature and place the rolled parotha on the pan. Leave it for a few seconds. Now turn it over and cook the other side for a few seconds. Turn it over again and cook for a further few seconds.

8. Now spread a teaspoonful of cooking oil on top of the cooking parotha and turn it over so that the oiled side is underneath. Spread the other side similarly with cooking oil and turn again to cook the second side. Continue cooking until both sides of the parotha are light brown. Remove the parotha from the pan and place it in a dish.

9. Cook all the parothas in this way.

LASSI

This is a yoghurt drink often served at meals. It may be served sweet or salty dependent on personal preference. For this recipe you need a whisk.

Ingredients   *Serves 4*

8 fl oz (250ml) natural fresh yoghurt
10 fl oz (300ml) water
½ tsp salt or 1 tsp sugar

Method   *Preparation and cooking time: 35 mins.*

1. Mix the yoghurt, water and salt (or sugar) in a large jug and whisk together for approximately 5 minutes.

2. Leave the mixture called lassi, to cool in the fridge for about 30 minutes.

3. Serve cold.

SAFFRON ALMOND MILK

This is sometimes served at night, just before going to bed. Try it instead of some other night time drink.

Ingredients   *Serves 4*

40 fl oz (1200ml) milk
A pinch of saffron
½ oz (10g) almonds, finely chopped

Method   *Preparation and cooking time: 30 mins.*

1. In a large pan, mix the milk and the saffron. Bring the milk to the boil, lower the heat and let the milk simmer very gently for about 20 minutes.

2. Add the almonds and simmer for a further 5 minutes. Serve hot or cold. Sugar may be added, dependent on taste.

8 SWEETS

DRY SWEET VERMICELLI

This is a sweet dish served as a dessert. It is not served in restaurants and therefore well worth trying at home.

Ingredients   *Serves 4*

3 oz (85g) sugar
15 fl oz (450ml) water
6 oz (170g) vermicelli
2 oz (55g) ghee
½ tsp ground cardamom
½ tsp nutmeg
1 oz (25g) almonds, finely chopped

Method   *Preparation and cooking time: 40 mins.*

1. Mix the sugar and water and bring the mixture to the boil.

2. Cook the vermicelli and ghee together, on a very low heat, stirring continuously, until the vermicelli turns golden brown. This usually takes about 15 to 20 minutes.

3. Add the sugar syrup, cardamom and nutmeg and stir well. Bring the mixture to the boil, reduce the heat and simmer gently until the water has evaporated. This will usually take about 15 minutes.

4. Transfer the contents to a serving dish and garnish with almonds. Serve while hot.

KHEER
(Rice pudding)

This is a sweet dish, similar to the traditional English rice pudding. It is usually served as a dessert and can be served hot or cold dependent on choice.

Ingredients   *Serves 4*

4 oz (110g) patna rice, or long grain white rice
10 fl oz (300ml) water
30 fl oz (900ml) milk
A pinch of saffron
3 oz (85g) sugar
¼ tsp ground cardamom
¼ tsp ground nutmeg
1 oz (25g) almonds, finely chopped
1 oz (25g) pistachios, finely chopped

Method   *Preparation and cooking time: 1 hr.*

1. Wash the rice and add the 10 fluid ounces of water.

2. Bring the water to the boil.

3. Reduce the heat, cover the pan and simmer gently for about 8 minutes, until the water has evaporated. Add the

milk and saffron. Bring it to the boil. Reduce the heat. If the mixture starts sticking to the bottom of the pot, lower the heat further. Simmer gently for about 30 minutes stirring every 5 to 7 minutes.

4. Add sugar and simmer gently for a further 15 minutes stirring every 5 to 7 minutes.

5. Switch off the heat. Place the cooked rice pudding in serving dish.

6. Garnish with ground cardamom, nutmeg, chopped almonds and pistachios.

GULAB JAMAN

This is a very sweet dish, often served as a dessert after a hot curry. It can also be served at parties or with high tea. It may be served hot or cold dependent on personal preference. For this recipe you need a deep frying pan or wok.

Ingredients   *Makes about 30 gulab jamans*

1 lb (450g) sugar
20 fl oz (600ml) water
8 oz (225g) gulab jaman powder or milk powder
1 oz (25g) self raising flour
1 oz (25g) plain flour
¼ tsp ground cardamom
¼ tsp ground nutmeg
2 oz (55g) melted butter
A pinch of saffron or 5 to 7 drops yellow food colouring
½ oz (10g) fine desiccated coconut
4 fl oz (120ml) milk
20 fl oz (600ml) cooking oil, for frying

Method   *Preparation and cooking time: 1 hr. 20 mins.*

1. Place the sugar in a pan, add the water and bring it to the boil. Lower the heat and simmer gently for about 5 minutes.

2. Place the gulab jaman powder (or milk powder) in a mixing bowl. Add the self raising flour, plain flour, ground cardamom, nutmeg, melted butter, saffron (or food colouring) and coconut. Mix well, adding milk gradually; thus turning the mixture into a soft dough. Divide the dough into about 30 equal parts and shape each into a smooth round ball.

3. Heat the oil in a wok or deep frying pan to a temperature such that when a crumb of bread is thrown into the oil, it browns within 15 seconds. Now reduce the heat to a simmer. Place the gulab jaman, four at a time, in the work and fry until the balls turn dark brown. Remove them from the oil and place them on a kitchen towel.

4. After all the gulab jaman have been fried, transfer the sugar syrup to a serving dish and add the gulab jaman. Leave the gulab jaman soaking in the syrup for about 30 minutes before serving.

5. If you like them cold then leave the gulab jaman in the syrup, for about 30 minutes in the fridge. If you like them hot then heat the syrup and the gulab jaman for about 10 minutes.

BESAN BARFI

(Gram flour fudge)

This is another dessert dish. It is not as sweet as gulab jaman and is served cold. It tastes very much like fudge and can be stored for up to 1 week after cooking. It can also be served at high teas or picnics. For this recipe you need a deep frying pan or wok.

Ingredients   *Serves 4*

4 oz (110g) sugar
4 fl oz (120ml) water
8 oz (225g) gram flour
4 oz (110g) ghee
4 oz (110g) gulab jaman powder or milk powder
5 drops yellow food colouring or
   a pinch of yellow food colouring powder
¼ tsp ground nutmeg
¼ tsp ground cardamom
1 oz (25g) almonds, finely chopped

Method   *Preparation and cooking time: 4 hrs. 40 mins.*

1. Place the sugar and water in a pan and bring the mixture to the boil. Simmer gently for about 8 or 9 minutes.

2. Sieve the gram flour into a wok or deep frying pan and add the ghee. Cook the mixture on a very low heat, stirring continuously, until the flour is golden brown.

3. Add the gulab jaman powder (or milk powder) and cook for another 2 minutes, stirring continuously.

4. Now add the sugar syrup. Stir continuously over a very low heat until the mixture is thick and sticky, very much like jam.

5. Remove the mixture from the heat, add the colouring, nutmeg and cardamom powder and mix well. Place the mixture in a greased tray. Garnish with almonds and leave it to cool down. While the mixture is still warm, cut it completely through, into cubes like fudge. Leave it to set for a further 4 hours. Separate the cubes.

6. This dessert is served cold.

CARROT HALVA
(A sweet carrot dessert)

This is a sweet and tasty carrot dish. It can be served hot or cold and this makes it more flexible.

Ingredients   *Serves 4*

12 oz (340g) carrots
3 fl oz (90ml) water
¼ tsp ground cardamom or 3 whole cardamoms, crushed
A pinch of saffron
6 fl oz (180ml) milk
2 oz (55g) sugar
1 tsp melted unsalted butter or ghee
1 oz (25g) almonds (skinless)

Method   *Preparation and cooking time: 2 hrs. 40 mins.*

1. Peel, and then grate the carrots.

2. Mix the grated carrots, water, cardamom and saffron in a large pan. Bring the water to the boil and then lower the heat. Cover the pan, and simmer gently for about 1 hour stirring every 10 to 15 minutes.

3. Add the milk and sugar and simmer for a further 1 hour on a low heat.

4. Add the butter or ghee, and evaporate the milk on a gentle heat. This usually takes about 15 minutes, and at the end you are left with very little liquid in the carrots.

5. Transfer the contents to a serving dish and decorate with the almonds. Serve either hot or cold.

KULFI
(Indian ice cream)

Kulfi is the Indian version of ice cream. It is very sweet and like most Indian desserts very heavy in calories. Most

Indian children love kulfi.

Ingredients *Serves 4*

20 fl oz (600ml) full cream milk
10 fl oz (300ml) condensed milk
2 oz (55g) skinless almonds, finely chopped
1 oz (25g) unsalted pistachio nuts,
    shells removed, finely chopped
3 oz (85g) sugar

Method *Preparation and cooking time: 5 hrs. 30 mins.*

1. Mix all the ingredients in a large pan, and bring the mixture to the boil.

2. Lower the heat, and let the mixture simmer for about one and a half hours, stirring every thirty minutes.

3. Transfer the mixture to an ice cube tray. Let it cool and then leave it to set, in a freezer, or the freezer compartment of a fridge for about 3 hours.

4. When you are ready to serve, remove the tray from the freezer, separate the cubes and serve in small fruit bowls.

SEMOLINA HALVA

Semolina halva is usually served in Sikh and Hindu temples. It is popular with vegetarians. It is a very sweet dessert and contains a large amount of fat.

Ingredients *Serves 4*

14 fl oz (420ml) water
4 oz (110g) sugar
¼ tsp ground cardamom
5 oz (140g) butter
4 oz (110g) semolina

Method   *Preparation and cooking time: 45 mins.*

1. Mix the water, sugar and cardamom and bring the mixture to the boil. Switch off heat.

2. In a large saucepan melt the butter. Lower the heat, and add the semolina. Stir continuously and cook until the semolina turns golden brown. This will usually take about 9 to 10 minutes.

3. Now add the water and sugar mixture, stirring continuously. Do this carefully, because, when first poured, the water will froth and may spit out of the pot. Make sure that you stir continuously, otherwise the mixture will become lumpy.

4. Increase the heat and bring the mixture to the boil. Lower the heat and cook for about a further 4 minutes stirring continuously. The mixture will be very thick and pasty.

5. Transfer the contents to a serving bowl and serve hot.

SAFFRON APPLE & ALMOND PUDDING

If you like apples then this dish is worth a try. It can be served with hot or cold custard, or cream.

Ingredients   *Serves 4*

1 lb (450g) eating apples
4 fl oz (120ml) water
4 oz (110g) sugar
A pinch of saffron
2 tsp cornflour mixed with 2 tsp water
4 oz (110g) almonds, finely chopped

Method   *Preparation and cooking time: 20 mins.*

1. Peel the apples and remove the cores. Cut the apples into chip-shaped pieces.

2. Mix the apples, water, sugar and saffron in a pan and bring to the boil. Lower the heat, cover the pan and let the

apples simmer for about 5 minutes.

3. Add the cornflour mixed with the water, mix well and let the mixture simmer for a further 2 or 3 minutes.

4. Transfer the contents to a serving dish and garnish with the almonds. Serve hot or cold (depending on taste) with cream or custard.

APPENDIX: SPICE NAMES

It is always cheaper to buy spices in larger packs rather than in small two ounce cartons. Most Indian spices are cheaper at Indian grocery shops and, if you know the Indian names, it makes it that much easier. So for the difficult spices here are the Indian names and their equivalent English names.

INDIAN NAME	ENGLISH NAME
Adhrak or Adhu	Ginger
Anardana	Pomegranate seeds
Atta	Chapatti flour
Badam	Almonds
Besan or Chana na loth	Gram flour
Dalchini	Cinnamon sticks
Dhanyia	Coriander
Haldi	Turmeric powder
Hing	Asafoetida
Jaifal	Nutmeg, whole
Jeera	Cumin seeds
Kala chana or Kale chole	Gram kichererbsen
Kali mirch sabat or Marri	Whole black peppercorns
Lachi or Alchee	Cardamoms
Lasan	Garlic
Methi	Fenugreek
Rai	Black mustard seeds
Soonf or Variari	Fennel seeds
Toovar or Har har di dahl	Hushed pigeon peas
Urad or Mahan di dahl	Black matape
White Chana or Chite chole	Chick peas

ENGLISH NAME	INDIAN NAME
Almonds	Badam
Asafoetida	Hing
Black matape	Urad or Mahan di dahl
Black mustard seeds	Rai
Cardamoms	Lachi or Alchee
Chapatti flour	Atta
Chick peas	White chana or Chite chole
Cinnamon sticks	Dalchini
Coriander	Dhanyia
Cumin seeds	Jeera
Fennel seeds	Soonf or Variari
Fenugreek	Methi
Garlic	Lasan
Ginger	Adhrak or Adhu
Gram flour	Besan or Chana na loth
Gram kichererbsen	Kale chana or Kale chole
Hushed pigeon peas	Toovar or Har har di dahl
Nutmeg, whole	Jaifal
Pomegranate seeds	Anardana
Turmeric powder	Haldi
Whole black peppercorns	Kali mirch sabat or Marri

MORE RIGHT WAY COOKBOOKS

In the same series

THE CURRY SECRET
The curry book with a difference! Kris Dhillon reveals the secret of *Indian Restaurant Cooking* and offers you the opportunity to reproduce that elusive taste in your own kitchen. Packed with recipes.

STEAMING!
Annette Yates' book is full of new recipes, combining healthy low-fat meals with traditional hearty fare. Cooking charts give steaming times for all kinds of food.

CHINESE COOKERY SECRETS
Deh-Ta Hsiung shares his life-long knowledge of Chinese *restaurant* cooking to help you successfully reproduce your favourite meals at home.

ICE 'N' EASY
Here, favourite cookery writer Annette Yates shows how to make luscious creamy concoctions, light-and-airy yoghurt mixtures and dairy-free ice creams, as well as sorbets, granitas and slushy drinks.

Uniform with this book

RIGHT WAY
PUBLISHING POLICY

HOW WE SELECT TITLES
RIGHT WAY consider carefully every deserving manuscript. Where an author is an authority on his subject but an inexperienced writer, we provide first-class editorial help. The standards we set make sure that every **RIGHT WAY** book is practical, easy to understand, concise, informative and delightful to read. Our specialist artists are skilled at creating simple illustrations which augment the text wherever necessary.

CONSISTENT QUALITY
At every reprint our books are updated where appropriate, giving our authors the opportunity to include new information.

FAST DELIVERY
We sell **RIGHT WAY** books to the best bookshops throughout the world. It may be that your bookseller has run out of stock of a particular title. If so, he can order more from us at any time – we have a fine reputation for "same day" despatch, and we supply any order, however small (even a single copy), to any bookseller who has an account with us. We prefer you to buy from your bookseller, as this reminds him of the strong underlying public demand for **RIGHT WAY** books. However, you can order direct from us by post or by phone with a credit card.

FREE
If you would like an up-to-date list of all **RIGHT WAY** titles currently available, please send a stamped self-addressed envelope to ELLIOT RIGHT WAY BOOKS, BRIGHTON ROAD, LOWER KINGSWOOD, TADWORTH, SURREY, KT20 6TD, U.K. or visit our website at www.right-way.co.uk